THE
PHILADELPHIA
EAGLES

The Eagles' first superstar, Davey O'Brien, was the prototypical quarterback. Since 1981, the National Collegiate Athletic Association (NCAA) has honored his memory by awarding the best quarterback in college football with the Davey O'Brien Award. (Courtesy of Historical Society of Pennsylvania.)

FRONT COVER: Philadelphia Eagles legends Norm Van Brocklin (left) and Chuck Bednarik (right) show off their respective game-day jerseys during a photograph shoot. (Photograph by Frank P. Montone; courtesy of Temple University Libraries.)

COVER BACKGROUND: Fans line up to see Eagles legend and University of Pennsylvania graduate Chuck Bednarik's pregame entrance at Franklin Field. "Concrete Charlie" spent his entire National Football League career with the Eagles (1949–1962) and was inducted into the Pro Football Hall of Fame in 1967. (Courtesy of Philadelphia Evening Bulletin Collection, Temple University Libraries.)

BACK COVER: Eagles fans sit in the notorious 700 Level of Veterans Stadium. (Photograph by George D. McDowell; courtesy of Temple University Libraries.)

THE
PHILADELPHIA
EAGLES

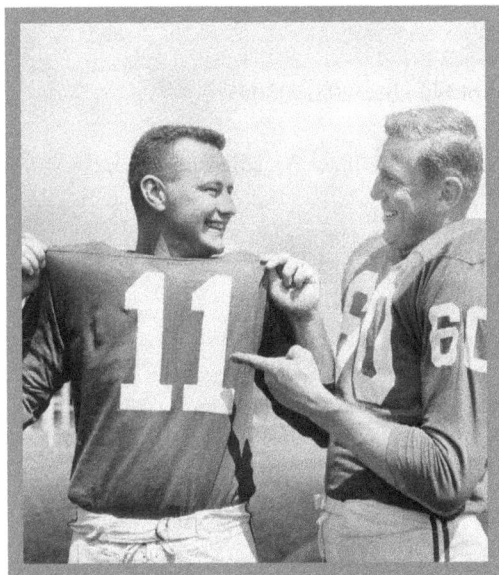

Brian Michael, Andrew Palagruto, and Andrew Weicker
Foreword by Ray Didinger

ARCADIA
PUBLISHING

To all the Eagles fans over the years, including our families

Published by Arcadia Publishing
Charleston, South Carolina

Library of Congress Control Number: 2021938096

For all general information, please contact Arcadia Publishing:
Telephone 843-853-2070
Fax 843-853-0044
E-mail sales@arcadiapublishing.com
For customer service and orders:
Toll-Free 1-888-313-2665

Visit us on the Internet at www.arcadiapublishing.com

CONTENTS

FOREWORD

For Philadelphia fans, the Eagles are more than a team. They are more than a rooting interest. They are family.

Yes, the Philly fans root for the other teams. They root for the Phillies, but they root for the Sixers and the Flyers too. When those teams won, the fans danced in the streets, and we all shared in the joy.

But with the Eagles, it is different. I have always believed that. We schedule our lives around them. We gather to watch them. Whether it is in the stands or in the living room, we are all there together. No one watches an Eagles game alone. We are all there. Mom, Dad, the kids, the grandparents, maybe an uncle, and an in-law or two. It is a family affair, and the Eagles are at the center of it.

So what you hold in your hands now is no mere sports book; it is a family album. It is a collection of all those moments, all those Sundays, all those trips to Franklin Field, all those tailgates at the Vet and the Linc, all those experiences that were about so much more than football.

I know the feeling because, like you, I lived it. I grew up going to Eagles games with my parents and grandparents. As a kid, I sat in my grandfather's Southwest Philly taproom and listened to the customers talk about the Eagles. The first time I saw my grandfather cry was when the Eagles beat Green Bay in the 1960 championship game. When Chuck Bednarik wrestled Jim Taylor to the ground on the final play, my grandfather's eyes filled with tears just the way mine did when I hugged my son after the Eagles won Super Bowl LII.

Again, it is family.

This is not a record book. It is not a book filled with statistics and box scores and the fine print of Eagles history. This is a book of images, of memories and emotions that resonate across the generations. Like a family album, it walks you through decades in a warm and personal way. It will make you smile, and it may bring a tear to your eye, but that is all part of being an Eagles fan, isn't it?

The author Eudora Welty once wrote: "A good snapshot keeps a moment from running away." This book is proof of that. There is a lot of speed in pro football—DeSean Jackson at the Meadowlands comes to mind—but one click of the shutter can freeze a moment for all time. The photographers who contributed to this book—some skilled professionals, others amateurs with a cell phone—have given Eagles fans of all ages something very special.

—Ray Didinger

ACKNOWLEDGMENTS

There are many people to thank for helping us revisit these cherished Eagles memories for fans to pass on to younger generations.

Once we got the green light from the good people at Arcadia, notably Jeff Ruetsche and Caroline Vickerson, the first person we called on was Ray Didinger. As Eagles fans know, his wealth of team knowledge is only outmatched by his kind heart. He has been an invaluable resource and inspiration for this project. The latest edition of his *Eagles Encyclopedia* made fact-checking a breeze, and his initial suggestion to speak to legendary Eagles photographer Ed Mahan proved immeasurable.

After several failed attempts to contact Ed, our research at the Frankford Historical Society introduced us to a mutual friend, Susan Couvreur (who also helped us find some never-before-seen Yellow Jackets photographs). Fortunately for us and fans, Ed has retained decades of photographs and negatives that allowed us to include even more exclusive images. We are extremely grateful to both for their generosity.

Throughout researching this book, we indirectly learned a lot about photography. Besides Ed and Susan, we have several professional photographers we would like to thank: Tom Briglia, Michael Spafford, Bob Novak, Dominic Savini, and the teams at Unique Photo and Icon Sportswire.

Well-maintained archives and hard working archivists from around the area and beyond also greatly assisted in our research, including Josué Hurtado, Temple University; Courtney Matthews, Library of Congress; Angela Schad, Hagley Museum and Library; Joaquin Moreland Sender and Andrew Williams, Historical Society of Pennsylvania; Timothy Horning, University of Pennsylvania; Bart Schmidt, Drake University; Josh Caster, University of Nebraska–Lincoln; and the folks at the City of Philadelphia Archives; Free Library of Philadelphia; and the Library Company of Philadelphia.

We were incredibly fortunate to have some of the Eagles family sharing their personal photographs with us, such as former Eagle Vince Papale, Melissa Pihos (daughter of Pete), Ken Safarowic (son-in-law of Chuck Bednarik), and Upton Bell (son of Bert).

We also would like to thank Peter Capolino, Mike Diaz from the Green Legion, and Vincent Rizzuto from Philly Sports Trips for invigorating the Eagles fan base and offering photographs from their collections. Crowd-sourced contributions from fans Lauren McLaughlin, Joe Cramphorn, Lisa Fazio, Mike Dillon, Elliott Gaskins, Sybil Katona, Barbara Barnes, and Jenny Pina made the cut, but hundreds more did not. We thank everyone who submitted an Eagles memory and gave us a peek into their personal fandom.

Along the way, we had several networking assists from Sal DeAngelis, J.P. Lutz, Khyber Oser, Rita Acchione, Rachel Micali, Pat Gallen, and Brian Harris. We appreciate them for helping to expand our reach in obtaining photographs.

We also would like to thank the team at Shibe Vintage Sports; Johnny Goodtimes in particular for creating PhillySportsHistory.com and donating material for captions; and Darren Nowicki, Glenn MacPherson, James Birrane, and Keenan Knight. Additionally, Sean Forman, his Philadelphia-based team behind Pro-Football-Reference.com, and all the authors in our bibliography deserve credit for keeping alive the stories of the past in a factual and accessible manner.

Finally, we can not forget about our friends and families. It's their fault we're Eagles fans, so they deserve as much credit as anyone.

INTRODUCTION

The game of football has a storied history in the city of Philadelphia. However, it was the Philadelphia Eagles who helped the game become a religion in the area. This story starts back in the 1880s, when Philadelphians would crowd the sidelines of high school games. Their interest in the sport grew even further when the annual Army-Navy football game came to town, and their love of the sport started to cement itself when college football became a mainstay with the University of Pennsylvania Quakers. There was something missing though, and that was a professional team that the city could cheer on. The Frankford Yellow Jackets were the first professional team in the city limits, but when they had to fold their franchise, it was Bert Bell who stepped up in 1933 and turned the Yellow Jackets into what are now the Philadelphia Eagles.

The first decade of Philadelphia Eagles football was rough to say the least. It took 11 seasons for the team to earn its first winning record, and for that to happen, it needed to merge the 1943 team with the Pittsburgh Steelers in order to field enough players due to the World War II draft. That merger season helped the franchise change its fortunes, and the Eagles continued to dominate for the rest of the 1940s, reaching three consecutive NFL Championship Games and winning two of them.

As the 1950s came along, the team was still competitive but could not reach that fourth NFL Championship Game fans desperately wanted. After a plummet in the standings towards the end of the decade, a ragtag group of teammates came together and compiled a historic 1960 campaign that resulted in the team beating the Vince Lombardi–led Green Bay Packers to win its third NFL Championship. This was the season Philadelphia fell in love with its football team.

Fans had their dedication and loyalty to the team tested many times following that 1960 season. It took the Eagles 18 years just to make the playoffs again. It was Dick Vermeil who finally stopped the bleeding and converted the team back into fierce competitors. With his emotional style of coaching, Vermeil was able to lead the Eagles to Super Bowl XV in 1980 but ultimately failed to bring the city its first Super Bowl victory. Just two seasons later, Vermeil was essentially forced into retirement (he cited burnout from the job as it was detrimental to his health). The team once again fell in the standings, and it would be a few more years before a coach was found to lead another turnaround.

The late-1980s and early-1990s Eagles became must-see television under the guidance of defensive guru Buddy Ryan. Ryan had collected a ferocious group of men that would terrorize opposing offenses. Not only did he have great defenders in Reggie White and Jerome Brown, but Ryan also had the ultimate weapon on offense—Randall Cunningham. Cunningham revolutionized the quarterback position with his dual-threat abilities, but countless injuries to him, along with the tragic death of Brown, prevented the team from making any deep playoff runs. Soon the Ryan era was over. The team would have a meager run through the rest of the 1990s; however, a positive change made at the end of the decade charted a new course for the franchise.

With the team having a head coach vacancy after the 1998 season, the Eagles made the curious move of making the relatively unknown Packers quarterbacks coach Andy Reid their next leader. With the help of a new franchise quarterback, Donovan McNabb, Reid was able to take the Eagles to the playoffs in just his second season. From there, the team consistently improved, later appearing in four straight NFC Championship Games. It took that fourth NFC Championship for the team to finally win and advance to Super Bowl XXXIX, where it fell just four points shy of bringing home that elusive Lombardi Trophy. This tenure was the longest extended playoff exposure the franchise had ever had, as the team ended up making the playoffs in nine of Reid's 14 seasons. However, since the team could not cross that Super Bowl hurdle under Reid, a divorce seemed to be the best case for both parties.

Replacing Reid would not be easy, but the team decided to hire a collegiate offensive whiz in Chip Kelly. Kelly's first season took the league by storm, as his innovative offense led to entertaining games and a division title for the team. Since he did so well early on, he was given more power from ownership to make the team how he saw fit. However, the power became too strong for Kelly. His ego made him trade star players like LeSean McCoy and ditch other Pro Bowlers like DeSean Jackson, as he thought his system could allow any player to succeed. That hubris was his downfall. The team failed to make the playoffs the following two seasons, and he was soon headed out of town.

After the Kelly fiasco, the franchise looked toward Doug Pederson, an Andy Reid protégé, to lead it back to the playoffs. Pederson did that and much, much more. In 2017, Pederson pushed all the right buttons with his players, and it resulted in a fun and magical season that ended with the team winning its first Super Bowl, defeating the Patriots 41-33 on February 4, 2018, in Super Bowl LII. The parade that culminated from the victory was 58 years in the making for Eagles fans, and generations of Philadelphians lined up and down Broad Street, across the Benjamin Franklin Parkway, and in front of the famed Philadelphia Museum of Art steps to cheer on the team and thank it for achieving the greatest sports feat in the city's history.

SELECT BIBLIOGRAPHY

Algeo, M. *Last Team Standing: How the Steelers and the Eagles Saved Pro Football during World War II.* Chicago: Chicago Review Press, 2006

Bowen, L. *Philadelphia Eagles: The Complete Illustrated History.* Minneapolis: MBI Pub., 2011.

Carlin, L., and P. Domowitch. *Bird's-Eye View: My Mostly Wonderful, Always Unforgettable Half-Century with the Philadelphia Eagles.* Chicago: Triumph Books, 2020.

Didinger, R., and R.S. Lyons. *The New Eagles Encyclopedia.* Philadelphia: Temple University Press, 2014.

Drabelle, D. "Heisman's Game". *Pennsylvania Gazette,* August 27, 2019. thepenngazette.com/heismans-game/ (Retreived February 16, 2021.)

Forbes, G. *Tales from the Philadelphia Eagles Sideline: A Collection of the Greatest Eagles Stories Ever Told (Tales from the Team).* New York: Sports Publishing, 2018.

Harris, B.H. *Frankford.* Charleston, SC: Arcadia Publishing, 2005.

Kowalski, E. *1960 NFL Champions: Relive the Philadelphia Eagles 1960 Championship Season.* Philadelphia: Sports Challenge Network, 2010.

Kowalski, E., and K. Safarowic. *Concrete Charlie: An Oral History of Philadelphia's Greatest Football Legend Chuck Bednarik.* Atlanta: Sports Challenge Network, 2009.

Loverro, T. *Eagles Essential: Everything You Need to Know to Be a Real Fan!* Chicago: Triumph Books, 2006.

Lyons, R.S. *On Any Given Sunday.* Philadelphia: Temple University Press, 2010.

Philadelphia Eagles: The Complete History. Mount Laurel, NJ: NFL Films, 2004.

Philadelphia Eagles: Greatest Games. Mount Laurel, NJ: NFL Films, 2009.

Philadelphia Eagles Franchise Encyclopedia. www.pro-football-reference.com/teams/phi/ (Retrieved February 16, 2021.)

Reese, M., and M. Eckel. *Merrill Reese: "It's Gooooood!"* Champaign: Sports Pub., 1998.

ABOUT

Shibe Vintage Sports has been keeping Philadelphia sports history alive with throwback apparel from name brands and local artists since 2013. Visit the shop at Thirteenth and Walnut Streets in Center City or ShibeSports.com.

Eagles Fan Frenzy is the premiere online fan community for the most die-hard Eagles fans. Join the club at: facebook.com/PhiladelphiaEaglesFrenzy.

1

THE BIRTH OF FOOTBALL IN PHILADELPHIA

BEFORE 1933

Philadelphia is an Eagles town, but it was not always that way. After the Civil War, the amateur game dominated the football landscape: high school rivalries were sparked and Thanksgiving Day opponents set. The Philadelphia Public League matchup between Northeast High School and Central High School has been played since 1892. William Penn Charter School and Germantown Academy started playing in 1887, and that game is considered by many to be the nation's oldest prep school rivalry.

At the collegiate level, this was the time when John Heisman was earning his stripes at the University of Pennsylvania. Not long after, Temple University hired the legendary Pop Warner to solidify its national reputation on the gridiron. Between 1894 and 1926, Penn, Lafayette, and Penn State won a combined 10 national championships. And after four years of alternating between New York and Maryland, the Army-Navy game found a neutral home in Philadelphia in 1899. Since then, Philadelphia has hosted the annual game more than any other city and has become synonymous with the armed forces tradition.

As amateur football captivated the city, the Frankford Athletic Association fielded a team of professionals in the newly formed NFL in 1924. With a home stadium at Frankford Avenue and Devereaux Street in lower Northeast Philadelphia, the Frankford Yellow Jackets won the 1926 NFL Championship. Unfortunately, the good times did not last long, and the team folded in 1931. However, from their ashes the Philadelphia Eagles were born.

Since the 1880s, Philadelphians have crowded to high school rivalry games, often on Thanksgiving Day. Some of the most storied matchups include Penn Charter v. Germantown (1887–present), Northeast v. Central (1892–present), and Frankford v. North Catholic (1928–2010). (Courtesy of Historical Society of Pennsylvania.)

Football has many great rivalries, but none can compare with the pride and pageantry of the Army-Navy game. From 1899 to 2021, Philadelphia played the role of neutral host for the schools' annual matchup 89 times. The Pennsylvania Railroad set up a temporary station at Municipal Stadium to transport upwards of 30,000 spectators on game day. (Photograph by D. Alonzo Biggard; courtesy of City of Philadelphia.)

Opened in 1926 for the Sesquicentennial International Exposition, Philadelphia Municipal Stadium hosted professional football games for the Philadelphia Quakers, the Frankford Yellow Jackets, and also the Eagles for four years. It was renamed John F. Kennedy Stadium in 1964 and hosted many huge concerts, including Live Aid in 1985. (Photograph by J. Victor Dallin; courtesy of Hagley Museum and Library.)

Franklin Field opened at Thirty-Third and Spruce Streets on April 20, 1895, and remains the oldest college stadium in the country. It is home to innumerable "firsts," including college football's first radio and television broadcasts, the first permanent horseshoe college stadium, and America's first double-decker stadium. (Courtesy of the City of Philadelphia.)

C.H. Schoff A.J. Bowser J.W. Adams H. Mellor H.W. Thornton F.C. Williams E. Wagonhurst R.R. Ammerman
Graham L. DePVail R.P. Griffith E.M. Church E.B. Camp J.W. Heisman J.H. Dewey
T.W. Huidekoper Captain T.F. Branson
A. Thompson

Philadelphia's first taste of football success on the national stage came courtesy of the University of Pennsylvania. The Quakers won or shared a national championship in the years 1894, 1895, 1897, 1904, 1907, 1908, and 1924. (Courtesy of University Archives and Records Center, University of Pennsylvania.)

John Heisman played and coached at Penn. His innovative and creative approach to the game was memorialized in his 1922 book *Principles of Football*. He is responsible for introducing the center snap, the audible "Hike/Hut" signal, coded directions, and offensive shifts as well as suggesting the legalization of the forward pass. (Courtesy of University Archives and Records Center, University of Pennsylvania.)

In 1903, the original wooden stands were replaced by a brick horseshoe to increase capacity to over 78,000. Here, a packed house watches the visiting Penn State Blue Band on October 20, 1928. (Photograph by J. Victor Dallin; courtesy of Hagley Museum and Library.)

After several successful seasons dominating local competition, Temple University football sought to grow its program by inaugurating a new 34,000-person stadium for the fall of the 1928 season. Located on Cheltenham Avenue in West Oak Lane, Temple Stadium hosted two Eagles games, including a 64-0 victory over the Cincinnati Reds in 1934. The Eagles also held training camp here before the 1936 and 1937 seasons. (Courtesy of Philadelphia Evening Bulletin Collection, Temple University Libraries.)

Heading into the 1933 season, Temple lured larger-than-life coaching icon Glenn "Pop" Warner from Stanford with a generous five-year, $75,000 contract. His innovative style solidified the Owls on a national stage—the 1934 team was undefeated. Pop finished with a record of 31-18-2 over six seasons and is the namesake for the nation's largest and oldest youth football program. (Courtesy of Philadelphia Evening Bulletin Collection, Temple University Libraries.)

College football also thrived in the region just outside Philadelphia with Penn State, Villanova, Lafayette, Lehigh, Princeton, Rutgers, Bucknell (then the University of Lewisburg), Dickinson, Franklin and Marshall, Haverford, Swarthmore, and more all fielding teams. National championships were shared or won by Penn State in 1911 and 1912 and by Lafayette in 1896, 1921, and 1926. (Courtesy of Historical Photograph Collection, Lafayette College.)

Philadelphia's first NFL team was the Frankford Yellow Jackets. An outgrowth of the Frankford Athletic Association, the team joined the NFL in 1924 and won the championship in 1926 with a 14-1-1 record, including 11 shutouts. (Photograph by Will S. Gibson; courtesy of the Frankford Historical Society.)

During their championship season in 1926, the Yellow Jackets battled the Green Bay Packers here on Thanksgiving. Due to Pennsylvania blue laws, home games were usually played on Saturdays, with Sundays reserved for worship and away games. (Courtesy of the Frankford Historical Society.)

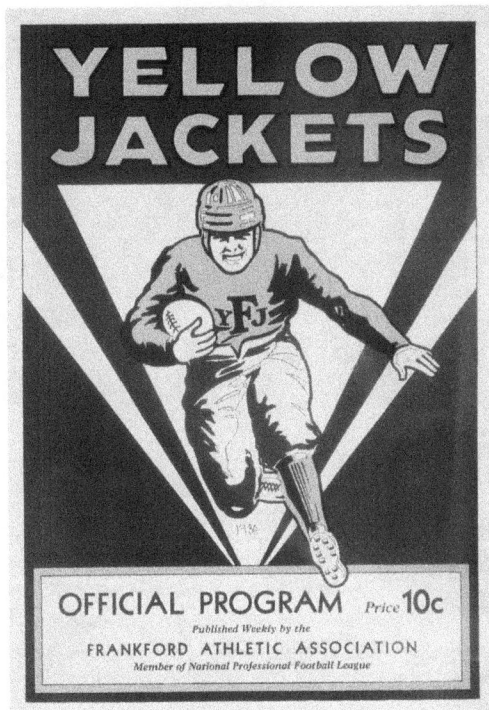

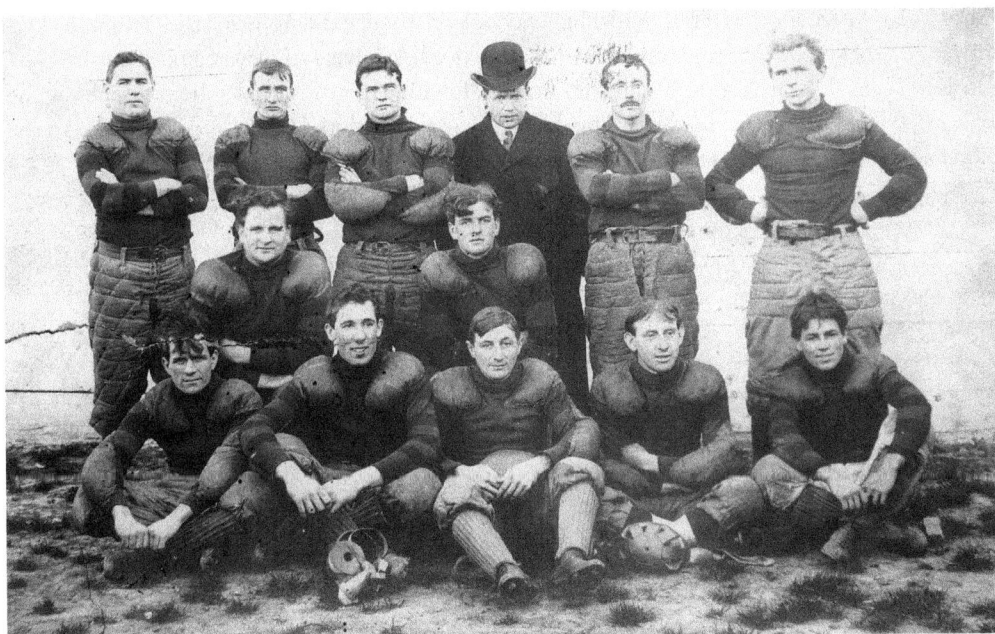

Guy Chamberlain played halfback for the Yellow Jackets and also coached. He was elected to the Pro Football Hall of Fame in 1965. Other famous Yellow Jackets include hall of famer William "Link" Lyman, Hap Moran, Two-Bits Homan, Charley "Pie" Way, Jug Earp, and Houston Stockton (grandfather of basketball great John Stockton). (Photograph by Will S. Gibson; courtesy of the Frankford Historical Society.)

AIRPLANE VIEW OF YELLOW JACKETS STADIUM AT OPENING GAME LAST YEAR. WERE YOU IN THIS PICTURE?

After the construction of Frankford High School on their existing field, the Yellow Jackets moved to a new $100,000 stadium located at Frankford Avenue and Devereaux Street in 1923. On July 27, 1931, a fire tore through the stadium, forcing the team to play home games at the Baker Bowl and Municipal Stadium. The damage, coupled with the Great Depression, led to the club folding after the 1931 season. (Courtesy of the Frankford Historical Society.)

The Philadelphia Quakers played one season in the rival American Football League. With coach Bob Folwell, they won the AFL Championship in 1926, giving the city two professional football championships in one year. (Courtesy of George Grantham Bain Collection, Library of Congress.)

As an industrial, medical, and legal hub for the nation, Philadelphia was dotted with amateur football clubs representing both neighborhoods and industries. The Pennsylvania Railroad football team competed from 1886 to 1905 against clubs like the Philadelphia Bank Clerks, Quaker City Wheelmen, Jefferson Medics, and USS *Alabama*, as well as local YMCAs, schools, and athletic associations. (Courtesy of Hagley Museum and Library.)

In 1925, the Pottsville Maroons (seen here) played an all-star team of Notre Dame players at Shibe Park in North Philadelphia. The Yellow Jackets complained to the league that their local rivals had infringed on their territorial rights by playing in the city. The NFL suspended the Maroons and gave the 1925 championship to the Chicago Cardinals. (Photograph by Will S. Gibson; courtesy of the Frankford Historical Society.)

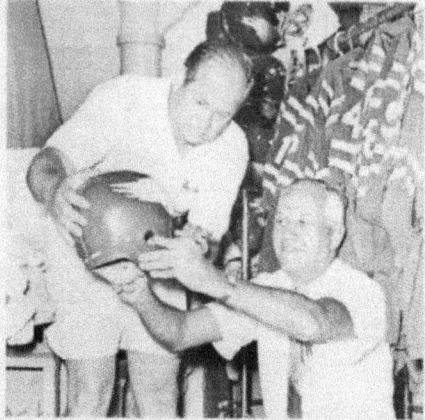

Philadelphia has a long tradition of sporting goods manufacturers. Companies like Pearson, A.J. Reach, Passon's, and Mitchell & Ness outfitted many teams around the country. (Courtesy of Andrew Palagruto.)

2

THE EAGLES HAVE LANDED

1933–1947

When the Yellow Jackets folded, a Main Line scion named Bert Bell purchased the rights to Philadelphia's NFL team for $2,500. He decided to drop the "Frankford" moniker in favor of the more inclusive "Philadelphia," in hopes of expanding the team's fanbase. The name "Eagles" was derived from the logo used for Franklin Roosevelt's National Recovery Administration. With the new brand in place, the Philadelphia Eagles played their first game in 1933 against the New York Giants at the Polo Grounds and lost 56-0. They finished their inaugural season with a record of 3-5-1. In fact, the Eagles' first 10 seasons were losing ones.

Bell hired Lud Wray as the Eagles' first head coach, and together they worked as the coaches, equipment managers, trainers, ticket takers, ushers, and newspaper reporters if one didn't show up for the game. Instead of hiring a secretary, Bell would also do that job himself. Wray was the head coach for three seasons in which the Eagles were a combined 9-21-1. After the Eagles' struggles under Wray, Bell took over as head coach for the next five seasons but did not fare much better with an overall record of 10-44-2.

Originally playing in North Philadelphia's Baker Bowl, the Eagles moved to Municipal Stadium (later renamed John F. Kennedy Stadium) in 1936 and then to Shibe Park in 1940. The early teams were composed of local college players from the Philadelphia area. The organization's first marquee player was Davey O'Brien, a five foot, seven inch quarterback and former Heisman Trophy winner. His NFL career spanned only two seasons with the Eagles, and he won All-League in 1939.

As the conflagration known as World War II raged and many NFL players were drafted, the NFL allowed short-staffed teams to merge for the 1943 season. The Eagles linked up with the Pittsburgh Steelers and were promptly christened the "Steagles" by local sportswriters. The officially named "Phila.-Pitt. Combine" finished the season 5-4-1, technically the Eagles' first ever winning season.

In 1944, the Eagles hired future Pro Football Hall of Fame coach Earle "Greasy" Neale. Neale named Tommy Thompson the starting quarterback, though he and the rest of the team were unaware Thompson was blind in one eye. Along with Thompson, Steve Van Buren, and Pete Pihos, the 1947 Eagles captured the East Division title with a record of 8-4. Though they lost to the Chicago Cardinals 28-21 in the NFL Championship Game, the seeds for success were beginning to take root.

The first name in professional football in Philadelphia—and in America for that matter—is undoubtedly De Benneville "Bert" Bell. After playing for the Penn Quakers, he bought the rights from the Philadelphia NFL franchise, the Frankford Yellow Jackets, in 1933 with $2,500 loaned to him by his wife, the actress Frances Upton. (Courtesy of Philadelphia Evening Bulletin Collection, Temple University Libraries.)

With Bert Bell as a new NFL franchise owner, his first order of business was renaming his team. As he was walking around the city, he saw a sign on Broad and Chestnut Streets for Franklin Delano Roosevelt's National Recovery Administration. The logo depicted an eagle, and he decided on using that for his franchise. That moment is when the Philadelphia Eagles were born. (Courtesy of Library of Congress Prints and Photographs Division.)

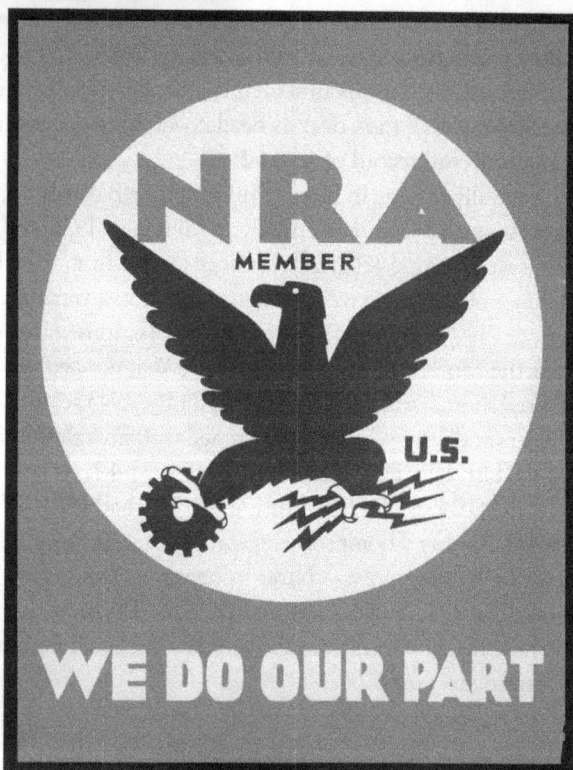

In 1946, Bell became the league's second commissioner. Some of Bert Bell's modern football innovations include sudden death overtime, the college draft, sharing television revenue, a pension plan for players, and the phrase "On any given Sunday." In 1939, the Eagles played the Brooklyn Dodgers in what was the first ever televised professional football game. (Courtesy of Upton Bell, Philadelphia Jockey Club.)

The Ritz-Carlton in Philadelphia hosted the first NFL draft on February 8 and 9, 1936. Bert Bell was the manager of the hotel owned by his family. With the first pick, the last-place Eagles selected Heisman-winning quarterback Jay Berwanger, who subsequently refused to report to camp. Bell was forced to trade him to the Chicago Bears. No players in this draft class ever played in the NFL. (Courtesy of the Free Library of Philadelphia.)

Philadelphia native Lud Wray stayed close to home when he attended the University of Pennsylvania, where he played football with Bert Bell and later coached the team (seen here). In 1933, Bell offered Wray the chance to be the Eagles' first head coach. Wray led the team to an abysmal 9-21-1 record in three seasons. When he was asked to take a significant pay cut to remain the coach, Wray quit, leaving Bell as the Eagles' next head coach. (Photograph by ACME News Pictures; courtesy of Brian Michael.)

Eagles head coach Greasy Neale was an outfielder for the Cincinnati Reds and briefly the Philadelphia Phillies before he started coaching in the NFL. He won the World Series over the infamous Chicago White Sox in 1919. He went on to coach the Eagles from 1941 to 1950, including coaching two NFL Championship–winning teams. (Courtesy of George Grantham Bain Collection, Library of Congress.)

The Eagles lost their first ever game 56-0 against the New York Giants at the Polo Grounds on October 15, 1933. Their first victory was a 6-0 win over the Cincinnati Reds on November 5, 1933. Many players were local products like Dave Smukler (center), known as the "Temple Terror." (Courtesy of Philadelphia Evening Bulletin Collection, Temple University Libraries.)

Tom "Swede" Hanson (white shirt) and his Temple football teammates are seen going over some strategy at a practice. Hanson went on to play for the Eagles in their inaugural 1933 season and later scored the first touchdown in franchise history. (Courtesy of Historical Society of Pennsylvania.)

The team's first marquee player was the Heisman-winning quarterback Davey O'Brien (21), seen here during an intra-squad scrimmage at St. Joseph's College in 1939. Standing a mere five feet, seven inches, O'Brien played two seasons (1939–1940) before joining the Federal Bureau of Investigation (FBI) as a special agent. He was awarded first-team All Pro in 1939 and second-team All Pro in 1940. (Courtesy of Historical Society of Pennsylvania.)

Davey O'Brien (center) takes a picture with Eagles owner Burt Bell (right) during an award presentation before the final home game of the 1940 season. Since O'Brien was his star player, Bell took out a $1-million life insurance policy from Lloyd's of London on him. (Courtesy of Historical Society of Pennsylvania.)

Frank Emmons (No. 44) is tackled by Max "Bananas" Krause of Washington after a four-yard pass from Davey O'Brien (No. 8). Even though Philadelphia finally had a pro football team, the product on the field took a while to develop. Due to the lack of star players on the team, the first decade of play saw an abysmal 23-82-4 record. (Courtesy of Historical Society of Pennsylvania)

After the 1940 season, the owner of the Pittsburgh franchise, Art Rooney (left), sold his team to young millionaire Alexis Thompson (center) and then became partners with Burt Bell (right). Thompson wanted to move his new team to Boston, but the league owners refused. The problem was solved by a franchise switch, with Thompson's Steelers moving to Philadelphia to become the Eagles and the Bell-Rooney Eagles going to Pittsburgh as the new Steelers. (Courtesy of Philadelphia Evening Bulletin Collection, Temple University Libraries.)

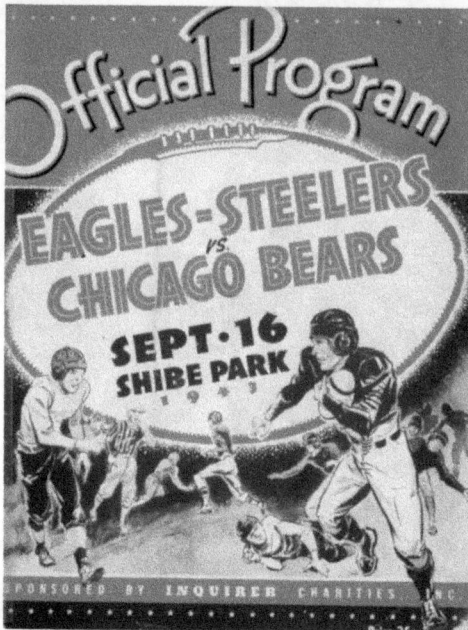

With the United States' involvement in World War II, most able-bodied men were drafted, leaving NFL rosters depleted. The Philadelphia Eagles and Pittsburgh Steelers decided to join forces for the 1943 season as the "Phil-Pitt Combine" but quickly became known as the "Steagles." The team set records on the field and in the stands, finishing above .500 for the first time and setting a new attendance record. (Courtesy of Andrew Weicker.)

Two Eagles, Theron Sapp (left) and Billy Barnes (right), leave with the 103rd Engineer Battalion of the Pennsylvania Army National Guard for two weeks of training at Camp Hill, Virginia. During World War II, two Eagles died while serving their country: Cpl. Mike Basca (France, 1944) and Lt. Len Supulski (training in Nebraska, 1944). (Courtesy of Philadelphia Evening Bulletin Collection, Temple University Libraries.)

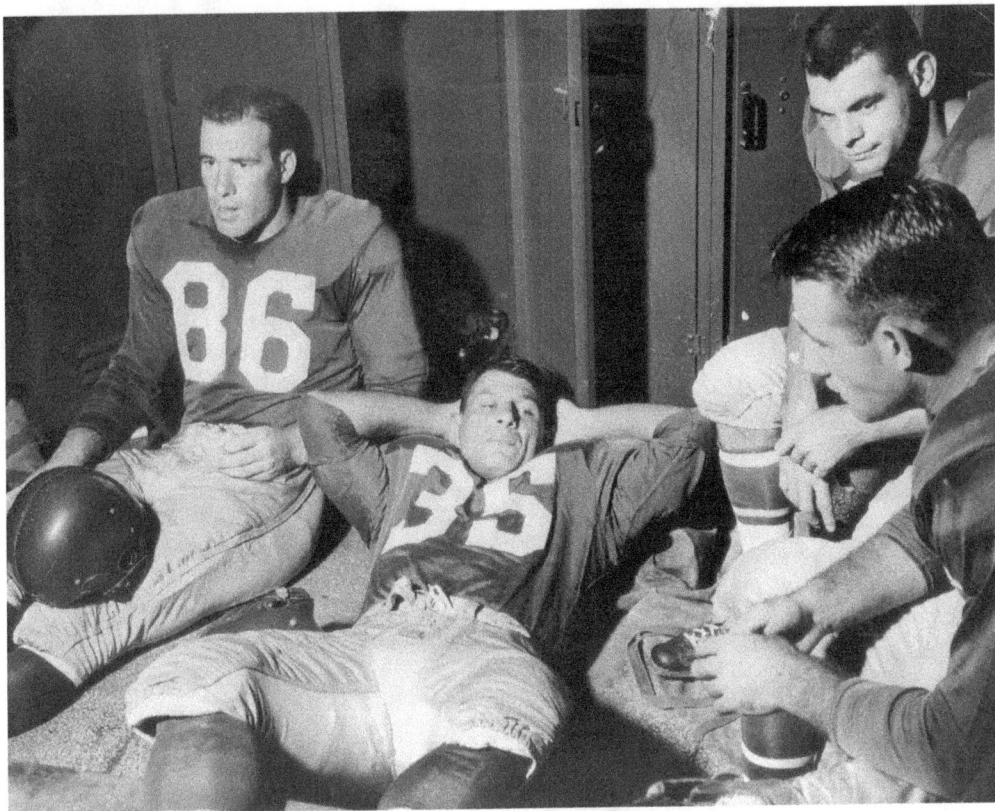

Before playing professional football, Pete Pihos (No. 35) was drafted into the US Army in 1944 and placed in the 35th Infantry Division, where he served under the famed Gen. George S. Patton. For his bravery overseas, Pihos was awarded both the Bronze Star and Silver Star. (Courtesy of Melissa Pihos.)

After fighting in Iwo Jima, Lt. Jack Sanders lost part of his left arm in an underwater explosion in March 1945. On August 17 that same year, he signed a contract with general manager Harry Thayer and the Philadelphia Eagles. In his first of only three appearances with the team, the US armed forces paid for 21,500 amputees to travel to and attend the game. (Courtesy of Historical Society of Pennsylvania.)

THE PHILADELPHIA EAGLES

The first Eagles training camp took place in 1933 at the Jersey Resort in Atlantic City. Here, running back Toy Ledbetter stretches his 200-pound frame a few years later in Hershey, Pennsylvania, where the Eagles set up preseason camp for 17 years after bouncing around local colleges and the Great Lakes region. (Courtesy of Philadelphia Evening Bulletin Collection, Temple University Libraries.)

Team physician Dr. Harrison Flippin examines halfback Leo Bledsoe prior to the 1945 season. Health checks were vital to the war effort, as most able-bodied men were drafted. At the time, NFL rosters were full of 4-F men with ailments ranging from ulcers to perforated eardrums who could not be drafted. (Courtesy of Historical Society of Pennsylvania.)

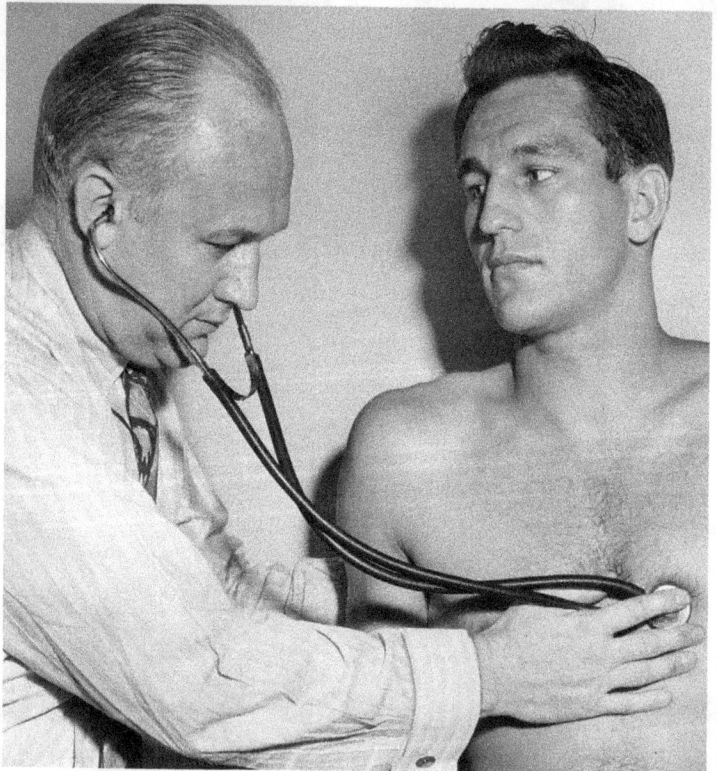

Like many early NFL teams, the Eagles' home field was at the local baseball stadium. For their first two seasons, they played at the Baker Bowl, the North Philadelphia home of the Phillies (seen here). Later on, they moved to Shibe Park—the magnificent home of the Athletics—from 1940 to 1958. The two stadiums were separated by just six blocks on Lehigh Avenue. (Above, courtesy of Philadelphia Evening Bulletin Collection, Temple University Libraries; below, courtesy of Housing Association of the Delaware Valley Photographs Collection, Temple University Libraries.)

The Eagles did not benefit just from using the Athletics' ballpark but also from manager Connie Mack's insistent lobbying to repeal Pennsylvania's blue laws. The blue laws made it illegal for sporting events to be played on Sundays. Thanks to Connie Mack, the commonwealth can now enjoy sports on Sundays. (Courtesy of George Grantham Bain Collection, Library of Congress.)

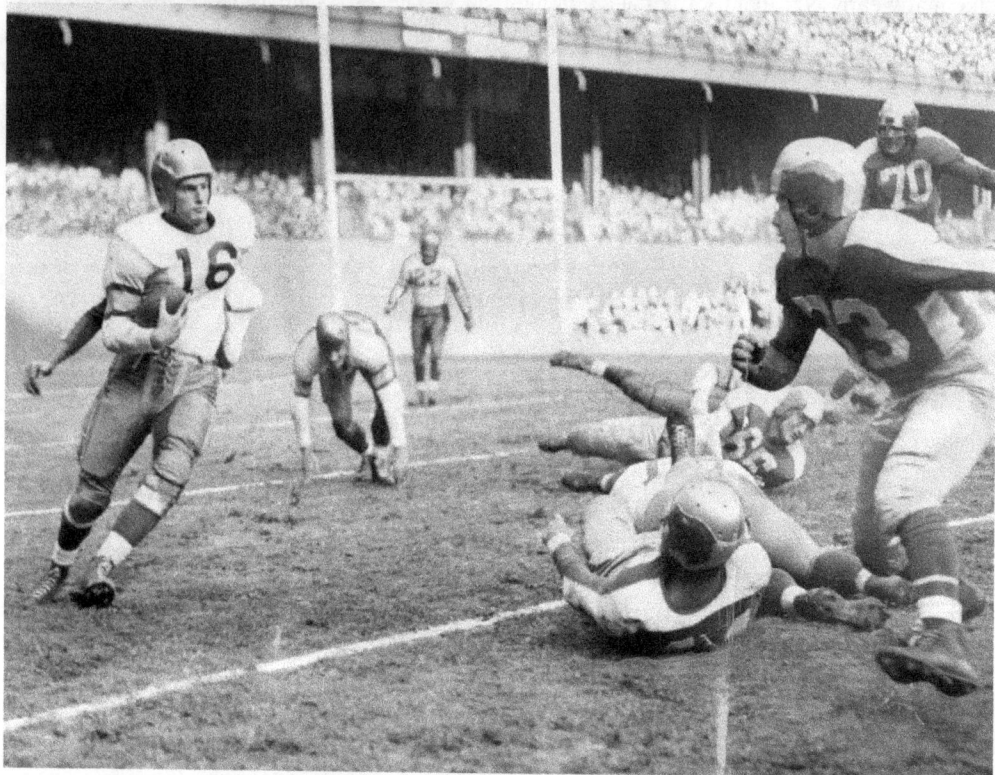

Eagles defensive back Russ Craft is pictured getting in position to tackle Boston Yanks back Howard Maley in a 1947 match held at Shibe Park. Craft spent eight years with the Eagles and was part of the 1948 and 1949 NFL Championship teams. He also played in two Pro Bowls while on the Eagles (1951–1952). (Courtesy of Philadelphia Evening Bulletin Collection, Temple University Libraries.)

THE EAGLES HAVE LANDED: 1933–1947

Ken Keller fumbles the football after being tackled by multiple Chicago Cardinals players in a 1956 matchup. The Cardinals recovered the ball and went on to win the game 20-6 at Connie Mack Stadium. The Eagles struggled mightily in that 1956 season, finishing sixth in their division with a 3-8-1 record. Glory was on the horizon though. (Courtesy of Philadelphia Evening Bulletin Collection, Temple University Libraries.)

Tackle Al Wistert is demonstrating an illegal use of the hands penalty on teammate and fellow offensive lineman Vic Sears. Both Eagles were named to the NFL's All-Decade Team for the 1940s. Wistert started his career with the Steagles and remained in Philadelphia as a part of the 1948 and 1949 NFL Championship teams. (Courtesy of Philadelphia Evening Bulletin Collection, Temple University Libraries.)

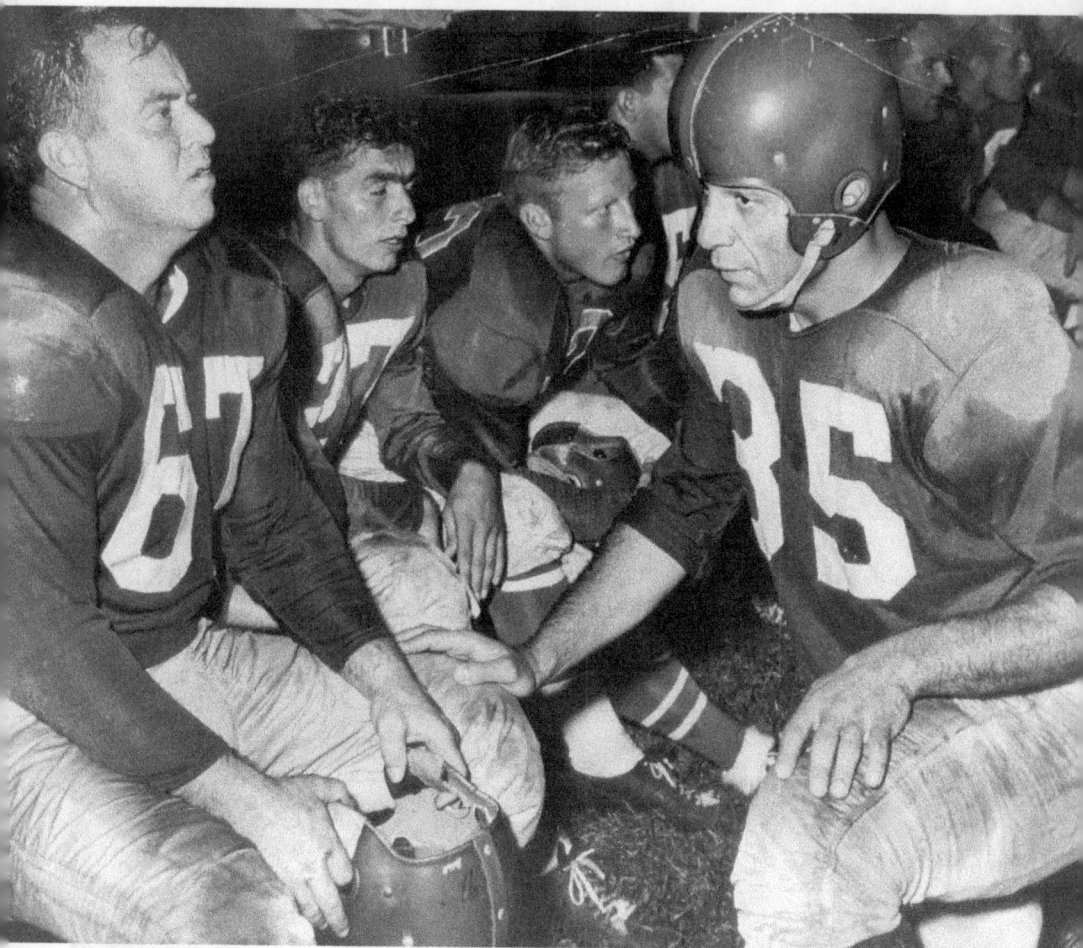

Multiple Eagles, including John Magee (No. 67) and Pete Pihos (No. 35), gather together in a locker room at halftime. With everyone sporting dirt and sweat stains, it is easy to picture how fierce the battles were on the gridiron that day. Magee and Pihos both spent their entire playing careers with the Eagles and were teammates from 1948 to 1955. (Courtesy of Melissa Pihos.)

3

NFL CHAMPIONSHIPS
1948 – 1970

In 1948, the Eagles won the NFL East Division for the second straight year with a record of 9-2-1 and went on to the NFL Championship, but this time they hosted the game at Shibe Park. The Eagles won the NFL Championship 7-0 against the Chicago Cardinals during a snowstorm. In 1949, they finished the season 11-1 and made it to a third straight title game. Steve Van Buren took charge for the Eagles offense by rushing for 196 yards on 31 carries in the NFL Championship Game against the Los Angeles Rams. The Eagles became the first and only team to win back-to-back NFL Championships each with a shutout.

After the 1949 season, the Eagles did not win the East Division for another decade. The team took another loss when Steve Van Buren suffered a career-ending injury. In 1958, Buck Shaw was hired as head coach, and he traded for quarterback Norm Van Brocklin. This move led to the Eagles getting back to the NFL Championship in 1960 with a 10-2 record. Behind Van Brocklin, the Eagles were able to overcome Vince Lombardi's Green Bay Packers 17-13 and brought a third NFL Championship to Philadelphia.

After their 1960 championship run, the Eagles turned to a new head coach in Nick Skorich and a new starting quarterback in Sonny Jurgensen. Jurgensen started 35 games from 1961 to 1963 and led the NFL in passing yards in 1961 and 1962. He is also tied for the longest touchdown pass in history at 99 yards. Even with Jurgensen's success under Skorich, the team only won five games combined from 1962 to 1963, and Skorich was fired.

Owner Jerry Wolman named Joe Kuharich as the new head coach and awarded him with an outrageous 15-year contract. He went on to trade away Tommy McDonald and Sonny Jurgensen, which quickly drew the ire of Eagles fans. After just five years and a combined record of 28-41-1, it was time for Joe to go.

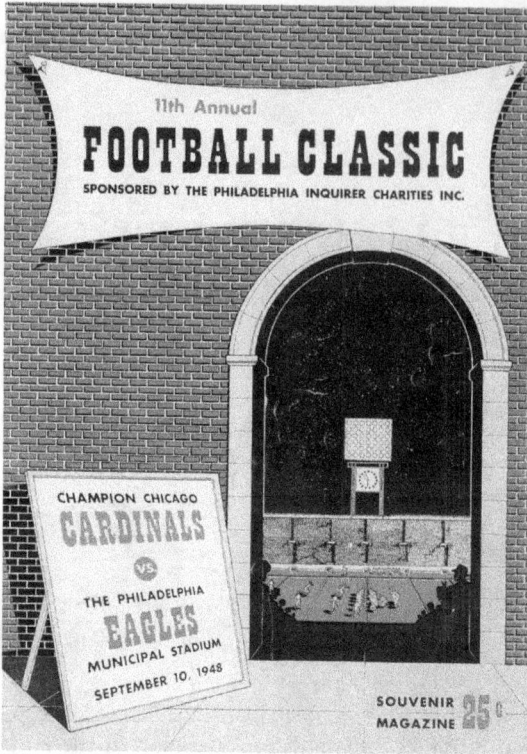

11th Annual

FOOTBALL CLASSIC

SPONSORED BY THE PHILADELPHIA INQUIRER CHARITIES INC.

CHAMPION CHICAGO

CARDINALS

vs.

THE PHILADELPHIA

EAGLES

MUNICIPAL STADIUM

SEPTEMBER 10, 1948

SOUVENIR
MAGAZINE 25c

Heading into this 1948 preseason game, the Eagles were coming off a heartbreaking 28-21 loss to the Chicago Cardinals in the previous year's NFL Championship Game. With an offense loaded with superstars and Greasy Neale's creative defense, the Eagles would not be denied in 1948 and 1949 with a combined record of 20-3-1. (Courtesy of Brian Michael.)

PHILADELPHIA EAGLES

Tommy Thompson   Quarterback   197 lbs.   6'1"   Tulsa

Tommy Thompson was blind in one eye from a childhood incident. Thompson led the Eagles to three consecutive NFL Championship appearances, including the 1948 and 1949 title-winning seasons. His 25 touchdown passes led the league in 1948, and he also led the team to victory in the championship game over the defending champion Chicago Cardinals in a snowstorm, avenging their loss in the previous year. (Courtesy of Ed Mahan.)

In the 1944 NFL draft, the Eagles selected Honduras-born Steve Van Buren, who went on to become one of the first superstar running backs in league history. He was given the nickname "Wham Bam" because he was six feet tall, 200 pounds, and a powerful runner. The hall of famer retired as the NFL record holder for both career rushing yards and rushing touchdowns. (Courtesy of Peter Capolino.)

PHILADELPHIA EAGLES

STEVE VAN BUREN

Legendary Eagles running back Steve Van Buren (left) and his brother Ebert Van Buren (right) played one year together in Philadelphia in 1951. Ebert was less successful than his brother, playing only three years. They are one of only three sets of brothers to have played for the Eagles at the same time. The others were Ty and Koy Detmer in 1997 and Shawn and Stacy Andrews in 2009. (Courtesy of Philadelphia Evening Bulletin Collection, Temple University Libraries.)

Known as the "Golden Greek," Pete Pihos played for the Eagles from 1947 to 1955 and only missed one game. He was selected All-Pro on offense six times and All-Pro on defense once. His excellence on the field led to him being elected to the Pro Football Hall of Fame in 1970. (Courtesy of Melissa Pihos.)

In a more tender moment, legendary offensive lineman Frank "Bucko" Kilroy is pictured playing football with his two teenage sons, Joe (left) and Frank Jr. (right). The Philadelphia native attended Northeast Catholic High School and Temple University before playing 13 seasons for the Eagles. Later a successful executive, he is credited with organizing the first scouting combine for the Eagles but is most often remembered for being one of the league's nastiest players. (Courtesy of Philadelphia Evening Bulletin Collection, Temple University Libraries.)

The 1948 championship was held at Shibe Park. Steve Van Buren rushed for the game's only touchdown in a 7-0 victory over the Chicago Cardinals. This cartoon, called "That Costly Fumble," features a St. Bernard with a football marked "N.L. Title" around his neck coming to the rescue of a Philadelphia Eagles football player buried by the snow. (Courtesy of Caroline and Erwin Swann Collection of Caricature and Cartoon, Library of Congress.)

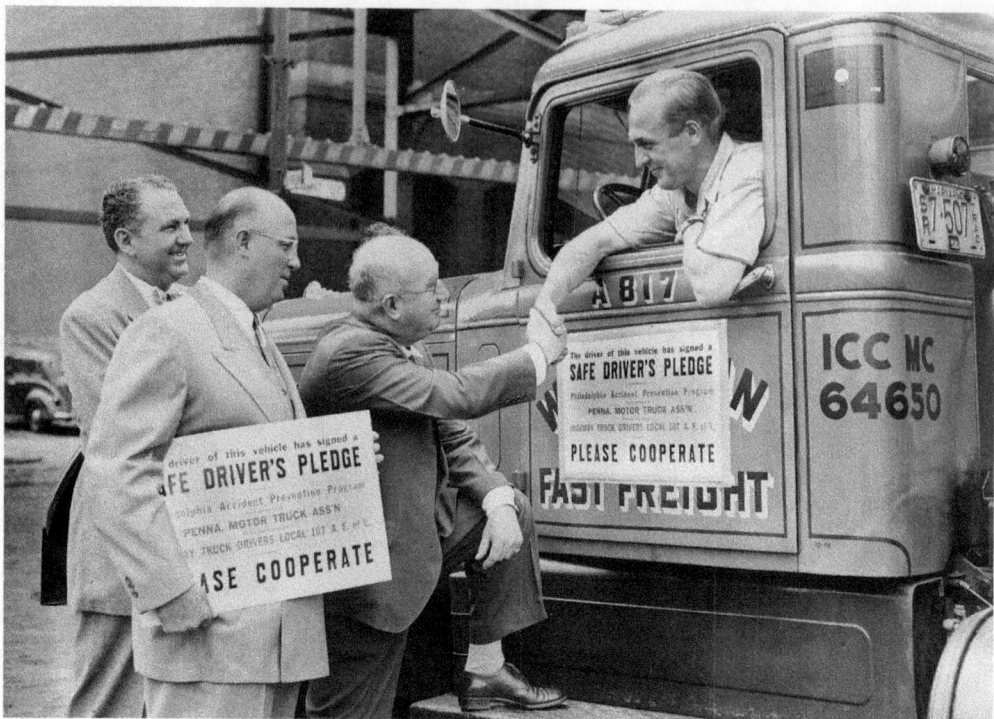

Alexis Thompson was the owner of the Eagles from 1941 to 1948. He sold them after they won their first championship to a group of 100 investors who were commonly referred to as the "Happy Hundred." The dysfunctional ownership group—led by trucker-turned-politico James P. Clark (holding sign)—managed to win two championships. (Courtesy of Philadelphia Evening Bulletin Collection, Temple University Libraries.)

In 1949, the Eagles' mini-dynasty continued, and on December 18, the team won its second consecutive NFL Championship by beating the Rams 14-0 at Los Angeles Memorial Coliseum. Steve Van Buren carried the Eagles to the win by rushing for 196 yards. The Eagles were the first—and so far only—team to win back-to-back championships by shutouts. (Courtesy of Peter Capolino.)

The president of the Philadelphia Chamber of Commerce, Ralph Kelly (left), is pictured here presenting a personalized "World Champs" football to the captain of the 1949 world champion Philadelphia Eagles, Al Wistert. The Eagles retired Wistert's No. 70 jersey, and in 2009, they inducted him into their hall of fame. (Courtesy of Philadelphia Evening Bulletin Collection, Temple University Libraries.)

Johnny Bright was the first African American man drafted by the Eagles in 1952. Selected in the first round, he instead elected to play professionally in Canada. The first black players for the Eagles were halfbacks Ralph Goldston and Don Stevens, selected later in that same draft. (Courtesy of Drake University Archives & Special Collections.)

Bob Brown was an intimidating force on the offensive live. Drafted second overall by the Eagles in 1964, he bulldozed paths for running backs for five seasons in Philadelphia. He earned five All-Pro and three Pro Bowl selections before being traded for Irv Cross following the 1968 season. In 2004, he was enshrined into the Pro Football Hall of Fame. (Courtesy of Archives & Special Collections, University of Nebraska–Lincoln Libraries.)

With the Eagles' popularity increasing, the team left Shibe Park, with its capacity of 39,000, for spacious Franklin Field, with room for over 60,000 fans. Before games, wide receiver Tommy McDonald would rub his fingers against the brick exterior for extra traction to assist in catching the ball, particularly during cold-weather games. (Courtesy of Peter Capolino.)

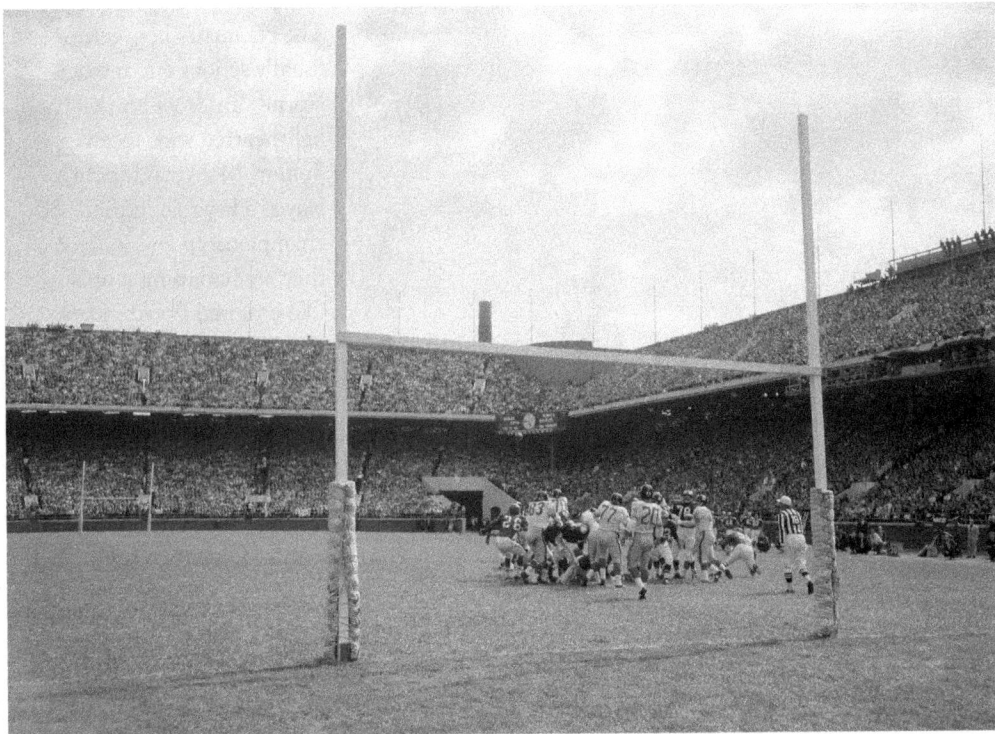

After the Eagles moved to Franklin Field, attendance skyrocketed, even though they had an overall record of 41-45-2 between 1958 and 1970. They may have an overall losing record at Franklin Field, but the team also won the 1960 NFL Championship Game there as well. In 2014, the team returned to the University City stadium for a preseason training session for fans. (Courtesy of Philadelphia Evening Bulletin Collection, Temple University Libraries.)

On October 11, 1959, Bert Bell died while attending a Eagles-Steelers game at Franklin Field. That may seem scripted by Hollywood: he once owned both teams, and the land Franklin Field was built on was donated by his family. This is his son Upton, also an NFL executive, revisiting the location. (Courtesy of Upton Bell.)

The chemistry between usually serious quarterback Norm Van Brocklin (left) and lighthearted wide receiver Tommy McDonald (right) played a key role in the 1960 championship season. Here, they are hamming it up at the Old Original Bookbinders. The team enjoyed dining there because the restaurant offered players and their families a free dinner after every shutout. (Courtesy of Philadelphia Evening Bulletin Collection, Temple University Libraries.)

Linebacker Chuck Bednarik (left) and quarterback Norm Van Brocklin (right) share a pregame conversation. These two veterans would help the team hand Vince Lombardi his only playoff loss in the 1960 NFL Championship. Both are enshrined in the Eagles Hall of Fame and Pro Football Hall of Fame. (Courtesy of Philadelphia Evening Bulletin Collection, Temple University Libraries.)

Chuck Bednarik is dripping wet after soaking his head in a water pot during training camp in Hershey in 1959. Outside of the 17 years in Hershey, the Eagles regularly held preseason camp at local colleges, among them West Chester and Lehigh Universities, which most frequently hosted the summer sessions. (Courtesy of Philadelphia Evening Bulletin Collection, Temple University Libraries.)

To say the 1960 Eagles got off to a slow start would be an understatement. They were blown out 41-24 by the Browns in Week 1 and barely beat the expansion Cowboys 27-25 in Week 2. Yet the scrappy bunch regrouped and pulled off six dramatic come-from-behind wins in the fourth quarter that season. No surprise then, this team produced three general managers and 11 head coaches. (Courtesy of LOOK Magazine Photograph Collection, Library of Congress.)

After losing to the Browns in the 1960 opener, the Eagles got revenge four weeks later on a game-winning 38-yard field goal by Bobby Walston (seen here). Walston spent 12 years (1951–1962) in Philadelphia catching passes and kicking field goals. He ended his career with 311 receptions and 46 touchdowns as a receiver. As a kicker, he has 80 field goals and 365 extra points made. He was enshrined into the Eagles Hall of Fame in 2018. (Courtesy of Philadelphia Evening Bulletin Collection, Temple University Libraries.)

PHILADELPHIA EAGLES

NORM VAN BROCKLIN QB

The Eagles acquired veteran quarterback Norm Van Brocklin from the Los Angeles Rams in 1958. "Dutch" was determined to win another championship in Philadelphia. After being named the franchise's first NFL Player of the Year in 1960, he abruptly retired. He immediately became the head coach of the expansion Minnesota Vikings after a handshake deal to coach the Eagles fell through. (Courtesy of Ed Mahan.)

Pete Retzlaff played his entire career with the Eagles (1956–1966). He held the franchise records for receptions (452), yards (7,412), catches in a season (66), and yards in a season (1,190). He was also selected to five Pro Bowls (1958, 1960, 1963, 1964, and 1965), twice first-team All-Pro, and twice second-team All-Pro. (Courtesy of Ed Mahan.)

PETE RETZLAFF   OFFENSIVE END   PHILADELPHIA EAGLES

After retiring from the NFL, Retzlaff went back to the Eagles to serve as the team's vice president and general manager from 1969 to 1972. He is enshrined in the Eagles Hall of Fame, and his No. 44 has been retired by the team. (Courtesy of Philadelphia Evening Bulletin Collection, Temple University Libraries.)

Here, Clearance Peaks (No. 26), Don Oaks (No. 77), and Billy Barnes (No. 33) are sitting on the bench as Sonny Jurgensen (No. 9) and Tommy McDonald (No. 25) approach the sideline in front of a packed Franklin Field in 1961. (Courtesy of Philadelphia Evening Bulletin Collection, Temple University Libraries.)

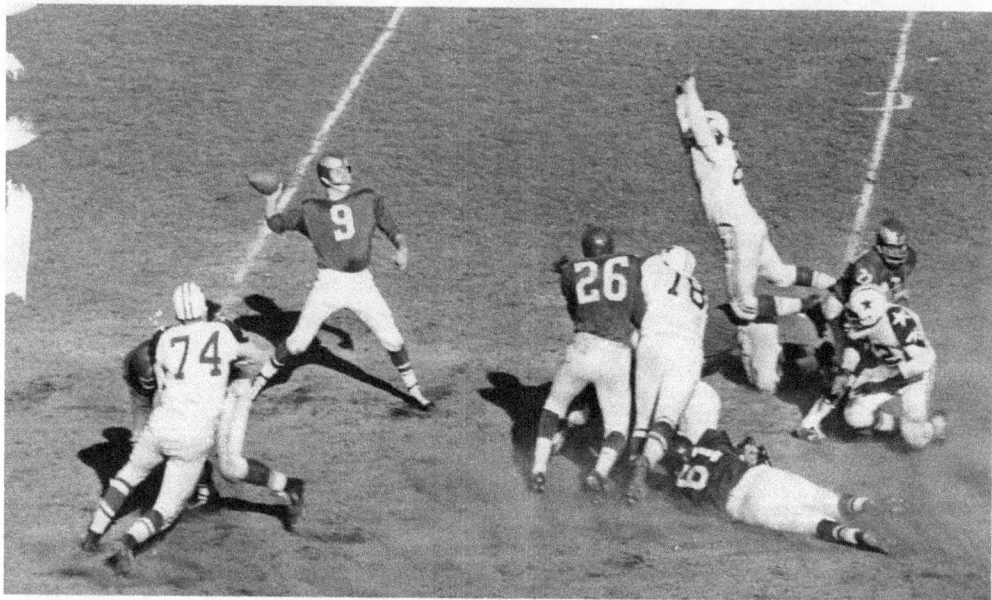

Sonny Jurgensen, who replaced Norm Van Brocklin as starting quarterback in 1961, is pictured here launching a deep pass against the Dallas Cowboys on November 26, 1961. It was just the third game between these eventual rivals, with the Eagles winning the first three. When Jurgensen left Philadelphia after the 1963 season, he had the second most passing yards (9,639) and passing touchdowns (76) in franchise history. (Courtesy of Philadelphia Evening Bulletin Collection, Temple University Libraries.)

FRANK BUDD   OB   5'10"   172   Villanova

Before Frank Budd was drafted out of Villanova by the Eagles in 1962, he was already a household name. Budd competed in the Summer Olympics in Rome in 1960 as a sprinter. He earned the title as "fastest man in the world" by setting the record for the 100-yard dash at 9.2 seconds in 1961. (Courtesy of Ed Mahan.)

Tommy McDonald was the last player to play without an NFL face mask. He led the league in touchdown catches twice (1958 and 1961) and was a six-time Pro Bowler (1958–1962 and 1965). At the time of his retirement, McDonald had the second most touchdown receptions in NFL history (84). At five feet, nine inches and 172 pounds, he is the smallest player ever inducted into the Pro Football Hall of Fame. (Courtesy of LOOK Magazine Photograph Collection, Library of Congress.)

Fullback Clarence Peaks was the seventh overall pick for Philadelphia in the 1957 NFL draft and spent seven seasons with the Eagles and two seasons with the Pittsburgh Steelers. Here, he is shown running with the football as his fellow teammates block opponents in an early 1960s Eagles game. Over his nine-year NFL career, Peaks ran for 3,660 yards and 21 touchdowns while also catching 190 passes for 1,793 receiving yards. (Courtesy of Philadelphia Evening Bulletin Collection, Temple University Libraries.)

Timmy Brown spent most of his career with the Eagles (1960–1967). In 1963, he set an NFL record by single-handedly racking up 2,346 yards of total offense. While playing for the Eagles, Brown worked on his singing career by releasing five singles between 1962 and 1964. After his retirement from professional football, Brown also began a career in acting. He appeared in 17 films and television shows from 1970 to 2000. (Courtesy of Philadelphia Evening Bulletin Collection, Temple University Libraries.)

Eagles players form a circle on the field before a game on November 24, 1963, two days after President Kennedy was assassinated. NFL commissioner Pete Rozelle insisted the week's games be played, and the Eagles lost 13-10 to Washington in front of a somber Franklin Field crowd. (Courtesy of LOOK Magazine Photograph Collection, Library of Congress.)

Through six seasons and two Pro Bowls (1964 and 1965) with the Eagles, Irv Cross is considered one of the best cornerbacks in franchise history. Upon retirement, he went on to become the first African American to work full time as a sports analyst on national television when he joined CBS in 1971. (Courtesy of Ed Mahan.)

Tom Brookshier started at defensive back for the Eagles from 1953 to 1961. During that time, he recovered eight fumbles and had 20 interceptions. His playing career was cut short when he suffered a compound leg fracture in a 1961 game. Even though he appeared in just 76 games with the Eagles, his No. 40 was retired by the team. He soon after pursued a career in sports broadcasting, and he joined CBS as its lead color commentator. (Courtesy of Philadelphia Evening Bulletin Collection, Temple University Libraries.)

Linebacker Maxie Baughan cools himself off on the bench with a wet towel as temperatures in Philadelphia approached 90 degrees in late September 1961. Baughan was a rookie when the team won the 1960 NFL Championship. He was named to the Pro Bowl team five times in his six years in Philadelphia and was elected to the Eagles Hall of Fame in 2015. (Courtesy of Philadelphia Evening Bulletin Collection, Temple University Libraries.)

Minnesota Vikings linebacker Steve Stonebreaker (No. 82) unwisely throws a haymaker toward Eagles safety Don Burroughs (No. 45) in an October 28, 1962, matchup. Jimmy Carr (No. 21), Ben Scotti (No. 48), Maxie Baughan (No. 55), Chuck Bednarik (No. 60), Bobby Richards (No. 68), Joe Lewis (No. 71), Riley Gunnels (No. 74), and Gene Gossage (No. 79) were all close by to make sure that the scuffle did not get any worse. (Courtesy of Philadelphia Evening Bulletin Collection, Temple University Libraries.)

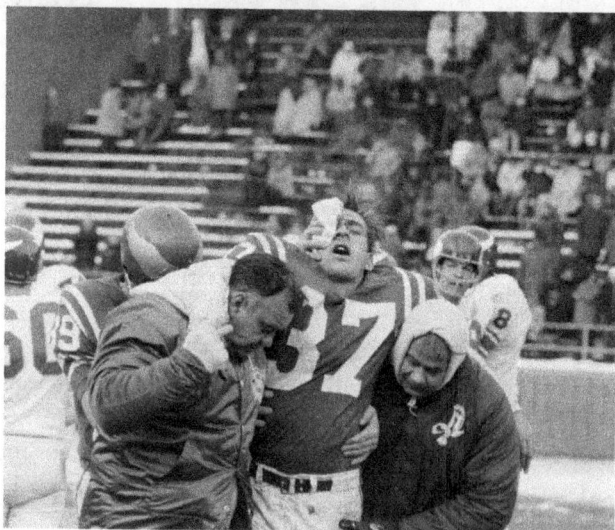

Following their 1960 NFL Championship win, the Eagles failed to reach the playoffs for the next 17 consecutive seasons. Peppered throughout the years were successful seasons by players such as Ted Dean, Norm Snead, Floyd Peters, Sam Baker, Harold Jackson, and wacky Tim Rossovich. Here Tom Woodeshick is being helped off the field in the final game of the 1968 season. (Courtesy of LOOK Magazine Photograph Collection, Library of Congress.)

In 1963, the "Happy Hundred" sold the franchise to Washington, DC, property developer Jerry Wolman. Originally from Shenandoah, Pennsylvania, the rags-to-riches-to-rags businessman made other investments in Philadelphia, including owning Connie Mack Stadium, the Spectrum, and the Flyers hockey team, but was forced to sell the Eagles when he lost his fortune building the John Hancock Center in Chicago. (Courtesy of Brian Michael.)

Before selling his sports empire, Wolman turned to friend and co-owner Ed Snider for help. He needed Snider to sell his share of the Flyers so they could unload the team and stabilize the finances for the Eagles. Snider refused, and Wolman was driven to bankruptcy. Snider then tried to buy the Eagles from Wolman for a song. Wolman needed the money but refused to sell to Snider, opting for Leonard Tose instead. Wolman and Snider never spoke again. (Courtesy of Temple Times Photographs Collection, Temple University Libraries.)

Profligate owner Jerry Wolman gave Joe Kuharich a whopping 15-year contract after his first year of coaching (1965). This photograph is from his final game as Eagles coach, a loss to the Vikings on December 26, 1968. (Courtesy of LOOK Magazine Photograph Collection, Library of Congress.)

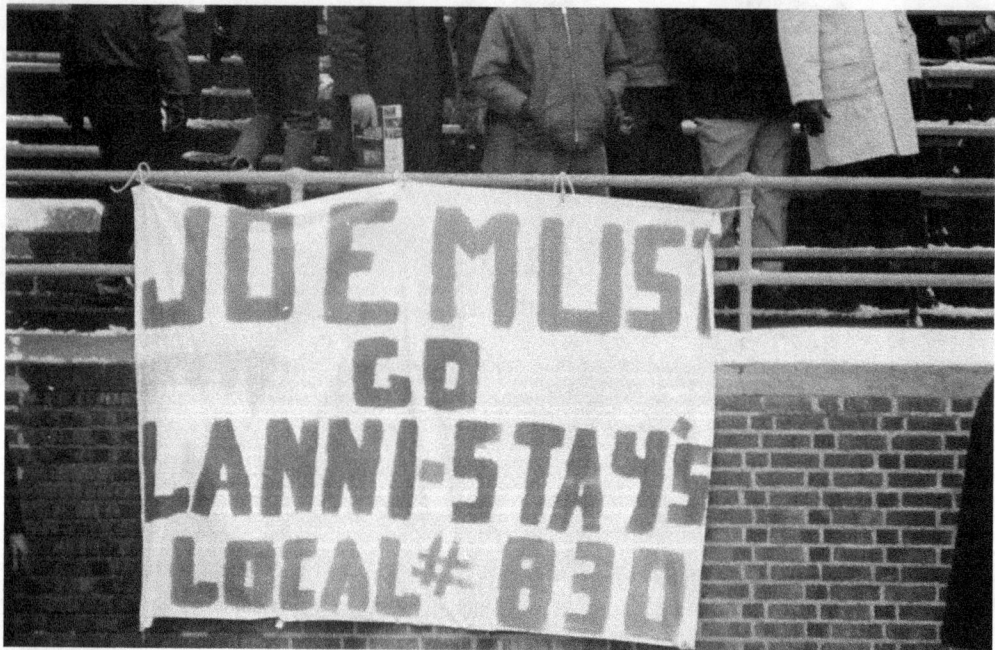

The media and fans despised Joe Kuharich due to him flaunting his contract and trading away star players like Tommy McDonald and Sonny Jurgensen. Fans flew planes, brought banners to the games, and held postgame rallies to get him fired. (Courtesy of LOOK Magazine Photograph Collection, Library of Congress.)

4

VETERANS STADIUM YEARS
1971–1996

With the emergence of Philadelphia as a football town, the time was right to give the Eagles a stadium that they could call their long-term home. Citizens voted for and ultimately approved the construction of a multipurpose stadium in South Philadelphia for the Philadelphia Eagles (and Phillies) to use.

At the time of its unveiling in 1971, the stadium was considered state of the art. However, the beloved Veterans Stadium would soon become notorious for different reasons. Whether it be the carpet-like turf, the colony of cats on rat patrol, or the municipal court installed underneath it, Veterans Stadium was nearly universally despised during much of its existence. But for Philly fans—particularly the uppermost 700 Level—it was home.

From a football standpoint, the Eagles' tenure at Veterans Stadium could be described as a roller coaster. The early part of the 1970s was not kind to the Birds, but their fortune changed when Dick Vermeil was hired to become head coach in 1976. By the 1980 season, his passionate approach had the team beating its archrivals, the Dallas Cowboys, in the NFC Championship Game to reach the first Super Bowl in franchise history. The Eagles lost to the Oakland Raiders in the big game and soon fell back to earth. Vermeil retired in 1982, citing burnout from his emotional coaching style, and left the Eagles scrambling for their next leader.

The Birds were near the bottom of the standings throughout most of the 1980s but started their next turnaround when Buddy Ryan came to town. Ryan's blue-collar attitude was adored by fans, and his monstrous defenses headed by the likes of Reggie White and Jerome Brown were feared across the NFL. Yet after three consecutive first-round playoff exits, Ryan was fired, and his successors saw little success as the new millennium dawned.

By the time it was completed, Veterans Stadium was one of the most expensive stadiums to date; it cost $60 million to build the new home of the Eagles and Phillies in South Philadelphia. Though it was considered modern at its launch, it quickly fell into disrepair and became known as a clunker of a stadium until it was imploded in 2004. (Courtesy of the City of Philadelphia.)

Due to construction delays, the opening of Veterans Stadium was postponed a year, and the Eagles had to move back to Franklin Field for the 1970 season. The schedule was already made, though, and the Eagles were playing a Monday night football game. The only problem was that Franklin Field did not have lights, so the Eagles chipped in to buy them. (Courtesy of the City of Philadelphia.)

This notorious Monday night football game was also the one where a drunken Howard Cosell (center) had to be removed from the broadcast booth at halftime after pregaming with owner Leonard Tose (left). (Courtesy of Ed Mahan.)

In its later years, "the Vet"—as it was affectionately known—was home to armies of feral cats left free to roam the building in hopes they could help curb the rat infestation. (Courtesy of Chamber of Commerce of the United States of America Collection, Hagley Museum and Library.)

Veterans Stadium is seen here in all its glory: a pregame scene from the 1980 NFC Championship Game versus Dallas. With a capacity of approximately 65,300 for football and 61,800 for baseball, the shared design was common among municipal stadiums during its era. (Courtesy of Ed Mahan.)

A former member of the "Happy Hundred," Leonard Tose bought the team for $16.1 million from Jerry Wolman in 1969. The flashy millionaire would commute to home games in a helicopter with Eagles wings painted on the sides. (Courtesy of Philadelphia Evening Bulletin Collection, Temple University Libraries.)

Tose's lavish spending on charities, divorce, alcohol, and gambling saddled him with enough debt that he considered moving the team to Phoenix in 1984. After a citywide backlash, he sold the Eagles in 1985 for $65 million—most of which was squandered. In his later days, he subsisted off donations by Dick Vermeil. (Courtesy of Brian Michael.)

The Eagles hired West Philadelphia native and Villanova graduate Jim Murray (left) in 1969 to their public relations staff. By 1974, Murray worked his way up to become the team's general manager. With the additions of Dick Vermeil and players like Ron Jaworski, Frank LeMaster, Wilbert Montgomery, Jerry Robinson, Roynell Young, and Mike Quick, Murray helped form an Eagles core that reached the postseason four times and claimed an NFC Championship. (Courtesy of Ed Mahan.)

Philadelphia Eagles teammates Bill Bergey (center) and Harold Carmichael (right) present a personalized Eagles jersey to Ray Kroc, the founder of McDonald's, at the grand opening of the first Ronald McDonald House on October 15, 1974. Fred Hill, a receiver on the team, had a five-year-old daughter diagnosed with leukemia. Hill, some teammates, owner Leonard Tose, and general manager Jim Murray all contributed to the Eagles Fly for Leukemia philanthropic program, which later helped to create the Ronald McDonald House. (Courtesy of Philadelphia Evening Bulletin Collection, Temple University Libraries.)

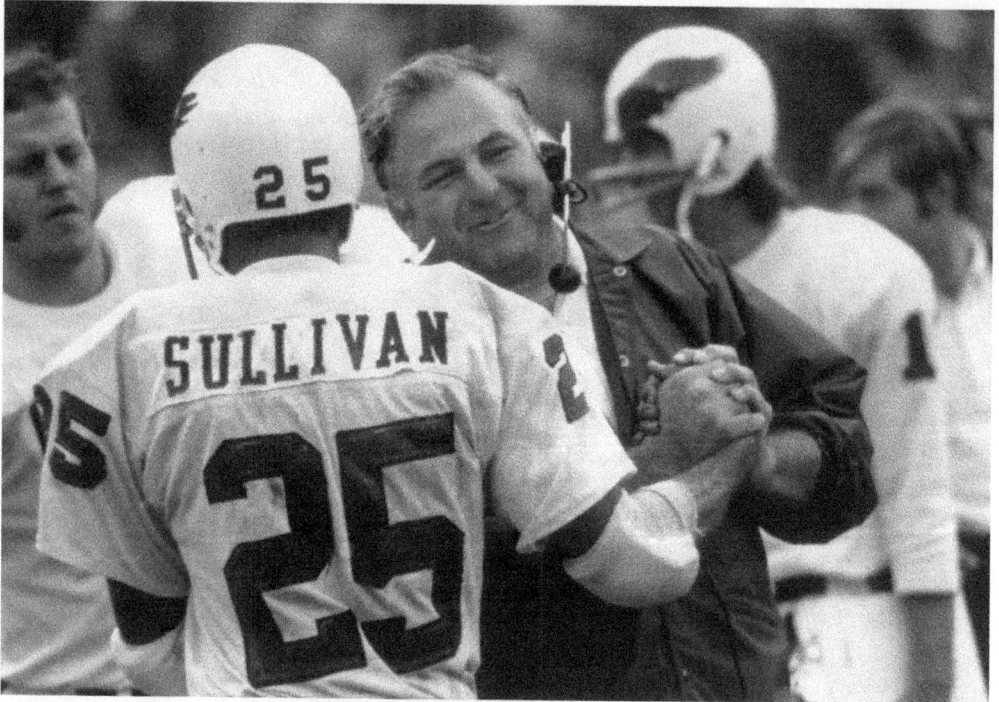

Pictured is coach Mike McCormack embracing running back Tom Sullivan. McCormack pushed the Eagles further down the NFL cellar in his three-year tenure as head coach. He traded away several draft picks, which forced his future replacement, Dick Vermeil, to find talent in free agency. (Courtesy of Ed Mahan.)

Dick Vermeil was like a father figure to many players, especially Ron Jaworski, and often teared up when talking about them. As the Eagles coach, he worked 20 hour days and slept in his office at the Vet. Citing burnout, he retired in 1982, but he returned to coaching 15 years later and won Super Bowl XXXIV with the St. Louis Rams. (Courtesy of Philadelphia Evening Bulletin Collection, Temple University Libraries.)

Like the 1960 team, the 1980 Eagles were a scrappy group who won games because they played as a family. Ron Jaworski (left) was the glue that helped keep the team stuck together. His lighthearted personality led to mischief like this scene in the locker room. (Courtesy of Brian Michael.)

The Bergey Bunch, also known as the Eagle linebackers, pose in Western garb, showing off the beards they grew as a symbol of their togetherness for the 1975 season. Pictured are, from left to right, Tom Ehlers, Frank LeMaster, John Bunting, Bill Bergey, Kevin Reilly, Dean Halverson, and Jim Opperman. (Courtesy of Philadelphia Evening Bulletin Collection, Temple University Libraries.)

One of the best moves the Eagles made in the 1970s was when they traded multiple first-round picks to acquire Cincinnati Bengals linebacker Bill Bergey. Bergey provided the veteran leadership the Eagles defense desperately needed to lead the team to Super Bowl XV. In his seven seasons as an Eagle, Bergey was selected to a combined five All-Pro teams and four Pro Bowl teams and is still remembered as one of the greatest linebackers in team history. (Courtesy of Ed Mahan.)

The Eagles held open tryouts in Dick Vermeil's first season as head coach. Only one player stood out: Vince Papale, a Delaware County native and Eagles season ticket holder. Papale earned a roster spot in 1976 and became one of the oldest rookies ever. His inspirational story was turned into the 2006 Disney movie *Invincible*. (Photograph by Ed Mahan; courtesy of Vince Papale.)

Fresh off the heels of a record-setting 63-yard field goal for the New Orleans Saints, Tom Dempsey signed with the Eagles in 1971. Dempsey was born without toes on his right foot or fingers on his right hand and had to wear a custom-made cleat to kick footballs. He spent four seasons kicking field goals and made 66 field goals, the ninth most in team history. He died in April 2020 from complications related to COVID-19. (Courtesy of Ed Mahan.)

Wade Key was just one of the unsung Eagles of the 1970s. He spent one season with the minor-league Pottstown Firebirds before joining the Eagles for 10 seasons. Key's play in the trenches helped him make the Eagles' 75th anniversary team. More unsung Eagles of the 1970s include Pro Bowlers defensive back Bill Bradley, tight end Charlie Young, left tackle Stan Walters, quarterback Roman Gabriel, quarterback Mike Boryla, and kick returner Wally Henry. (Courtesy of Ed Mahan.)

At the time of his retirement, Jerry Sisemore had played 156 games in an Eagles uniform, the fifth most in franchise history. The offensive lineman was a big part of the rebuild through the 1970s that led to the team's success in the late part of the decade and beyond. He was recognized for his excellent play with two Pro Bowl selections in his career. (Courtesy of Ed Mahan.)

Known as "Jaws" or the "Polish Rifle," Ron Jaworksi broke virtually every quarterback record in franchise history in his 10 seasons with the club, including wins (69), completions (2,088), passing yards (26,963), passing touchdowns (175), fourth-quarter comebacks (15), and game-winning drives (20). (Courtesy of Philadelphia Evening Bulletin Collection, Temple University Libraries.)

Eagles head coach Dick Vermeil is pictured talking with quarterback Ron Jaworski near the sideline during a break in a 1978 game against the Dallas Cowboys. Vermeil and Jaworski were in Philadelphia together from 1977 to 1982, leading the Eagles back to prominence. After missing the playoffs for 16 consecutive seasons, in 1978 the Eagles started a run of four straight appearances, including a trip to the Super Bowl. (Courtesy of Philadelphia Evening Bulletin Collection, Temple University Libraries.)

Eagles teammates Harold Carmichael (left) and Ron Jaworski (right) bicycle around Cooper River Park in Cherry Hill. Carmichael was the eventual winner of this race, using his long legs to help finish first. At six feet, eight inches, Carmichael is still the tallest receiver in NFL history. The 1980 NFL Man of the Year used his big frame to catch the most passes (589) and touchdowns (79) in Eagles history. After a long wait, he was finally inducted into the Pro Football Hall of Fame in 2020. (Courtesy of Philadelphia Evening Bulletin Collection, Temple University Libraries.)

Wilbert Montgomery made many contributions to the Eagles in the late 1970s and early 1980s, making him one of the best late-round draft picks in Eagles history. The Mississippi native was a sixth-round pick. His 6,538 rushing yards were the most in franchise history. His 1,512 rushing yards in 1979 were the most in a season in Eagles history. It was a record that lasted for over 30 years before LeSean McCoy broke it with 1,607 yards in 2013. (Courtesy of Ed Mahan.)

Herm Edwards (No. 46) enters the field at Veterans Stadium alongside his teammate Dennis Harrison (No. 68). Edwards enjoyed a nine-year career as a cornerback in Philadelphia. The straight talker later became a successful broadcaster and head coach. (Courtesy of the Library Company of Philadelphia.)

Edwards's most famous play as an Eagle became known as the "Miracle at the Meadowlands." Down 17-12 in the final moments of a 1978 game against the New York Giants, the Eagles were out of options with no time-outs left. However, Giants quarterback Joe Pisarcik botched his hand-off attempt to running back Larry Csonka, which resulted in a fumble. Edwards returned the fumble for a touchdown and gave the Eagles an unbelievable victory. The play helped spark a turnaround for the franchise; it made the playoffs that season for the first time since 1960 and two seasons later made the Super Bowl. (Courtesy of Ed Mahan.)

Whether through 8-mm film or tablet computers, players and coaches spend countless hours watching game footage, a practice pioneered by Greasy Neale. Shown here is hall of fame coach Sid Gillman, who was the quarterbacks coach for the Eagles under Dick Vermeil. (Courtesy of Ed Mahan.)

In one of the Vet's most memorable games, the Eagles hosted the rival Dallas Cowboys for the NFC Championship Game on chilly January 11, 1981. Wilbert Montgomery was questionable coming into the game due to collapsing at practice earlier in the week, but he exploded for a 42-yard touchdown on the second play of the game and put to rest any concerns about his health. The Eagles' 20-7 victory secured their place in Super Bowl XV. (Courtesy of Ed Mahan.)

Though they were the favorites to win, the Eagles suffered a disappointing loss in Super Bowl XV to the Oakland Raiders in New Orleans. Former Raiders coach and CBS analyst at the time John Madden was actually drafted by the Eagles as an offensive tackle in 1958. His playing career ended before it could begin, as he injured his knee in training camp and never played a game. (Courtesy of Ed Mahan.)

Marion Campbell spent 12 seasons with the Philadelphia Eagles in multiple roles, first as a player from 1956 to 1961. He rejoined the team as defensive coordinator in 1977 and was a big success at the position; the Eagles allowed the fewest points in the league in 1980 and 1981. Campbell was promoted to head coach when Dick Vermeil stepped down but could not find the same success in the new role. He never finished above fourth place in his three years in charge. (Courtesy of Ed Mahan.)

A rival professional football team known as the Philadelphia Stars took advantage of the Eagles' decline after the 1980 season due to aging veterans, front office dysfunction, and the 1982 NFL players strike. The well-run Stars were stocked with recognizable names both on the field (Ken Dunek, Sean Landeta, Kelvin Bryant, Carl Peterson, and John Bunting) and off (Jim Mora, Jay Wright, Leo Carlin, and Bill Kuharich). The Stars won the United States Football League (USFL) Championship in 1984 and 1985. (Courtesy of the City of Philadelphia.)

Norman Braman, a West Philadelphia native and Temple University alum, made his fortune in Miami as a car dealer. He bought the Eagles from Leonard Tose in 1985 for $65 million. Head coach Buddy Ryan would openly mock his boss by pejoratively calling Braman "the man in France" in reference to the owner's frequent vacations. In the end, Braman was thrifty when it came to free agency and allowed star players like Reggie White, Keith Jackson, Seth Joyner, and Eric Allen to leave the nest. (Courtesy of Temple University Libraries.)

On January 28, 1986, Eagles owner Norman Braman hired Buddy Ryan, the defensive coordinator of the Super Bowl–winning Chicago Bears, as the franchise's 17th head coach. Even as an Oklahoma native and former Army platoon sergeant, he quickly won the fans over with his blue-collar mentality and brutal honesty. Ryan finished his five-year stint with a winning record but a disappointing 0-3 result in the playoffs. Nonetheless, Ryan's Eagles are remembered fondly for finishing with an 8-2 record against the Cowboys. (Courtesy of Kevin Reese/Icon Sportswire.)

Often referred to as the "Ultimate Weapon," Randall Cunningham gave opposing teams nightmares with his arm and with his legs. Even though he was the quarterback, Cunningham led the Eagles in rushing from 1987 to 1990. Philadelphia made him the highest-paid quarterback in the league in 1989, signing him to a five-year, $15-million deal. He quickly rewarded the team with that investment, as he became the first Eagle to win NFL Offensive Player of the Year in 1990. Cunningham's legs were also utilized in the punting game; he holds two of the three longest punts in Eagles history, including an epic 91-yard punt in 1989, which remains the third-longest punt in NFL history. Although his No. 12 jersey does not hang in the rafters, the number is considered unofficially retired. Nobody in Philadelphia has worn that number since his departure after the 1995 season. (Courtesy of Kevin Reese/Icon Sportswire.)

Multiple Eagles linemen are seen practicing in the heat of summer as they prepare for another long season in front of them. Training camp is a great time for Eagles fans, particularly the young ones, to get a closer look at their heroes and maybe even get an autograph or a picture. (Courtesy of Temple University Libraries.)

As Harold Carmichael's career dwindled down, the Eagles needed a new No. 1 receiver. They struck gold when they selected Mike Quick in the first round of the 1982 NFL draft. Quick rapidly became an elite receiver, earning consecutive Pro Bowl selections from 1984 to 1988 while leading the league with 53 touchdowns during that span. In 1985, he tied an NFL record when he completed a game-winning 99-yard touchdown reception in overtime. Since 1998, Quick has provided color commentary on radio broadcasts of Eagles games. (Courtesy of Andy Lewis/Icon Sportswire.)

Fans (and opponents) of the Eagles were treated to consistent, high-quality defensive performances throughout the early 1990s. The 1991 "Gang Green" defense—widely regarded as one of the greatest in NFL history—finished top against the pass, rush, and overall. Here in 1995, the defense is seen stopping Emmitt Smith on three consecutive plays at the goal line. (Courtesy of Ed Mahan.)

After a brief stint with the USFL, Reggie White joined the Eagles and won Rookie of the Year in 1985. The eventual hall of famer averaged 15.5 sacks in eight years with the team. His departure through free agency—the first star player to do so in the NFL—represented a major victory for NFL players. (Courtesy of Cliff Welch/Icon Sportswire.)

Sadly, the Eagles lost Jerome Brown, their tenacious defensive tackle, in the 1992 offseason when he died in a car accident. The 1992 season was dedicated to "Bring it Home for Jerome," and the Eagles won a playoff game that season for the first time in 12 years. (Courtesy of Kevin Reese/ Icon Sportswire.)

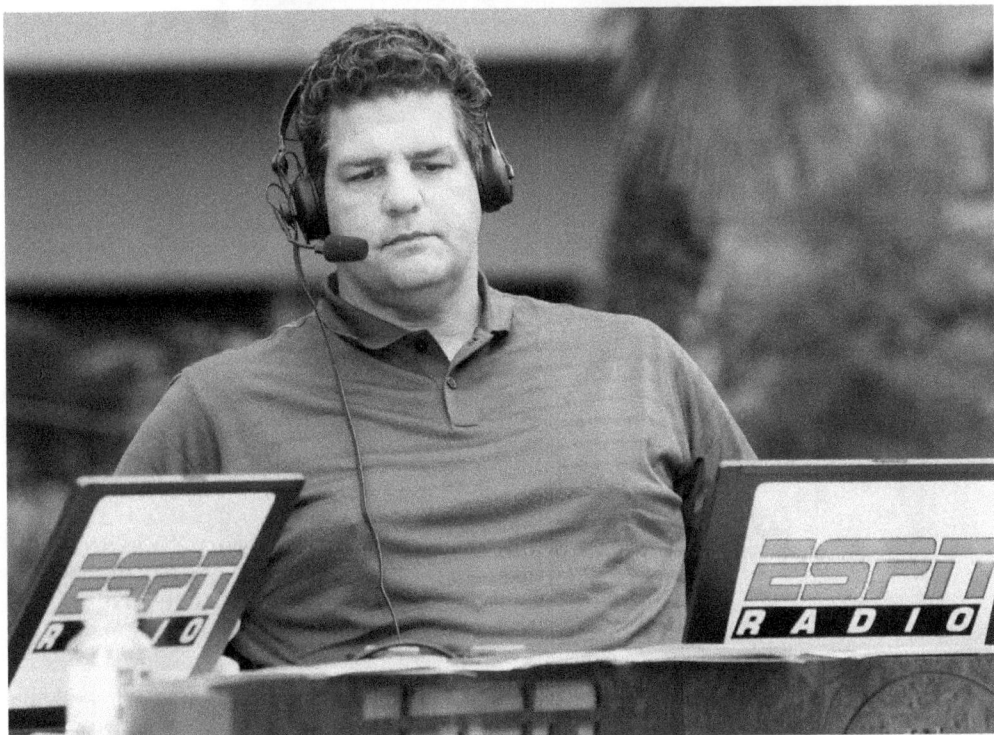

Mike Golic spent six seasons (1987–1992) in the trenches of the "Gang Green" defense, but he found even more success once his playing days were over in the form of broadcasting. In 2000, he joined Mike Greenberg to form *Mike & Mike*, an ESPN radio show that enjoyed a successful 17-year run. (Courtesy of Icon Sportswire.)

THE PHILADELPHIA EAGLES

Keith Byars, a versatile fullback for the Eagles, was able to run the ball like a running back and catch the ball like a receiver. He was one of the many underrated Eagles of his era. Linebacker Frank LeMaster, defensive end Dennis Harrison, tight end Keith Jackson, wide receiver Fred Barnett, running back Herschel Walker, kick returner Vai Sikahema, defensive end William Fuller, linebacker William Thomas, running back Ricky Watters, and wide receiver Irving Fryar were also key pieces for the team in those days. (Courtesy of Ed Mahan.)

Rich Kotite joined the Philadelphia Eagles as an offensive coordinator in 1990. In 1991, he became head coach when the team fired Buddy Ryan. With plenty of talent still left from Ryan's original roster, Kotite was able to lead the Eagles to 21 victories in his first two seasons. Once all of Ryan's drafted players started leaving in free agency, Kotite could not draft suitable replacements. Fans grew tired of Kotite after he went 8-8 in 1993 and told the media, "Hey, eight and eight is great." He was fired after the 1994 season. (Courtesy of Ed Mahan.)

In April 1994, Jeffrey Lurie bought the Eagles from Norman Braman for $195 million, which at the time was the most money spent on a sports franchise. The movie producer, seen hugging quarterback Rodney Peete after a 58-37 victory over the Detroit Lions in the 1995 Wild Card Round, brought a level of professionalism to the team and has owned it through arguably the most successful tenure in franchise history. (Courtesy of Ed Mahan.)

At the conclusion of his first season as owner, Jeffrey Lurie fired Rich Kotite. Lurie wanted to bring back Dick Vermeil, but the two could not come to a contract agreement. In 1995, Lurie hired Ray Rhodes, the first African American head coach in team history. The Mexia, Texas, native was known for his hard-nosed mentality and was a straight talker to the media. Rhodes would last four years in Philly, going 29-34-1. After a great start, going 10-6 and winning Coach of the Year in his first season, things went downhill rapidly, and he was fired after a disastrous 3-13 season in 1998. (Courtesy of Ed Mahan.)

5

THE "SO CLOSE, YET SO FAR" ERA

1997–2012

As the new millennium approached, so did a new era of Eagles football. With new owner Jeffrey Lurie, the franchise was ready to move forward and build something that had not been done in Philadelphia in over five decades—a consistently winning football team.

The first thing the team needed under its new ownership was a coach that could lead the team to the promised land and bring home a Lombardi Trophy. Lurie went on to hire Ray Rhodes, the first African American head coach in team history, to try to turn the franchise back on the right path. The team had early success under Rhodes, making the playoffs in his first two seasons. However, two consecutive losing seasons afterwards ultimately led to his departure. Tasked with finding another head coach, Lurie made a bold move in hiring a relatively unknown quarterbacks coach from Green Bay by the name of Andy Reid.

Over the next 14 seasons, Reid's team climbed the ranks and became a Super Bowl contender year in and year out as the Eagles entered their most successful era (from a winning percentage standpoint). His core of game-changers, including Donovan McNabb, Brian Westbrook, and Brian Dawkins, helped bring the team to four consecutive NFC Championship Games. They failed to make the Super Bowl in their first three attempts but finally cleared that hurdle in the 2004 season, when they advanced to Super Bowl XXXIX. Unfortunately, they ran into the New England Patriots, who were in the early stages of building their league-changing dynasty; the Eagles fell just four points shy of achieving ultimate glory.

In one last-ditch effort under Reid, the Eagles assembled a "Dream Team" in 2012 when they brought in several high-profile players from around the league. It quickly became a nightmare, and Eagles fans began to call for a new head coach to bring the city a Super Bowl.

Out of nine teams looking for a new head coach in 1998, only the Eagles chose to interview Green Bay quarterbacks coach Andy Reid. The Eagles brass were blown away by Reid's preparedness and quickly hired him. Reid went on to coach the Eagles through one of the best stretches in franchise history. He is one of only four coaches in NFL history to lead a team to more than 100 wins in a decade. (Courtesy of Thomas E. Briglia/PhotoGraphics.)

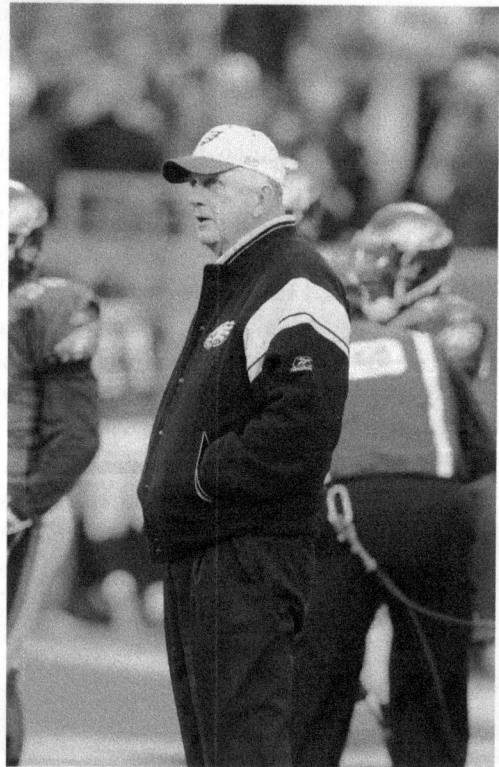

One of Andy Reid's first moves as Eagles head coach was to hire Jim Johnson to be the team's defensive coordinator. In 2001, Johnson's defense became just the fourth team in NFL history to hold opponents to 21 points or fewer in every game of a complete 16-game season. Johnson loved to blitz opposing offenses; from 2000 to 2007, the Eagles defense amassed 342 sacks, tied for first in the NFL during that time. (Courtesy of Thomas E. Briglia/PhotoGraphics.)

John Harbaugh was just one of a handful of assistant coaches that Andy Reid retained from Ray Rhodes's staff. He remained the special teams coach all the way through 2006 and then spent one season as the Eagles defensive backs coach before landing a head coaching gig in Baltimore and winning a Super Bowl. Harbaugh is one of many coaches on the "Andy Reid Coaching Tree" who went on to become a future head coach in the NFL, including Todd Bowles, Brad Childress, Leslie Frazier, Sean McDermott, Matt Nagy, Doug Pederson, Ron Rivera, Pat Shurmur, and Steve Spagnolo. (Courtesy of Ed Mahan.)

Jon Gruden came to Philadelphia in his early 30s to join the Eagles as offensive coordinator. The young hotshot was part of the Eagles staff from 1995 through 1997, with the team making two playoff appearances during that time. He left the Eagles in 1998 to become the head coach of the Oakland Raiders, and in 2002, he coached the Tampa Bay Buccaneers to their first Super Bowl championship. In 2009, he became a broadcaster and made a name for himself as the color analyst on *Monday Night Football*, but the coaching bug bit him again, and he rejoined the Raiders as their head coach in 2018. (Courtesy of Ed Mahan.)

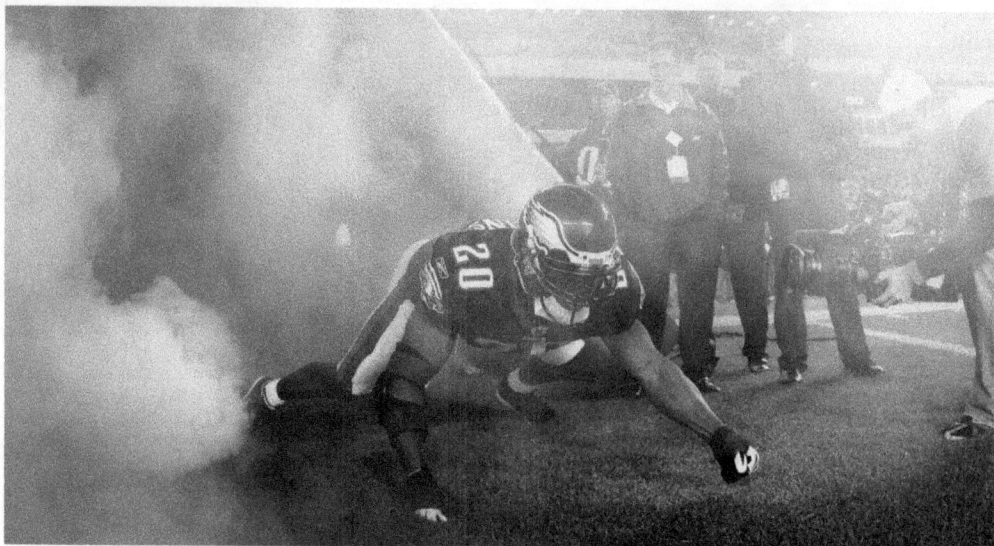

Ask any member of Generation X or millennials to name the first Eagles player that comes to mind, and almost all of them will say Brian Dawkins without hesitation. Dawkins, commonly known as "Weapon X," was the heart and soul of the Eagles defense in the early 2000s. The nine-time Pro Bowler is the only player in NFL history with at least 25 interceptions, 25 sacks, and 25 forced fumbles. (Courtesy of Icon Sportswire.)

Brian Dawkins was named a member of the NFL's All-Decade Team of 2000s and for good reason. His 221 regular-season games at safety are the second most in NFL history. He is also tied with Eric Allen and Bill Bradley for most interceptions in Eagles franchise history (34) and is still the only player in NFL history to have a "quadrafecta game" where he recorded a sack, a fumble recovery, an interception, and a touchdown reception. (Courtesy of Brian Garfinkle/ Icon Sportswire.)

Photo: Tom Briglia/PhotoGraphics

Even though he was booed by fans when he was drafted second overall in the 1999 NFL draft, Eagles fans quickly came around on Donovan McNabb. His legend started in 2000 when he accounted for 75 percent of the Eagles offense and finished second in MVP voting. Then in week 11 of the 2002 season, on the third play of the game, McNabb was sacked and injured his ankle. Thinking it was sprained (it was actually broken), he had it wrapped and returned to the game to throw four touchdown passes. After 11 seasons with the team, McNabb holds virtually every passing record in Eagles history: games played by a quarterback (148), passing yards (32,873), completions (2,801), attempts (4,746), and touchdowns (216). (Courtesy of Thomas E. Briglia/PhotoGraphics.)

With the Eagles lacking receiver talent for most of the 2000s, they had to turn to their running back, Brian Westbrook, for some help in the passing game. The Villanova University product set the Eagles single-season receptions record (90) in 2007—unusual for a running back—and held it for 11 seasons until Zach Ertz caught 116 passes in 2018. Through the 2020 season, the dual-threat running back is still the Eagles all-time leader in scrimmage yards (9,785) and all-purpose yards (10,700). For his contributions to the Eagles, he was selected to the 75th anniversary team and inducted into the team's hall of fame. (Courtesy of Thomas E. Briglia/PhotoGraphics.)

There was a time in the late 1990s and early 2000s when it may have sounded like Eagles fans would boo after positive running plays. In fact, they were yelling "DUUUUUCE!!!!!" to cheer on Duce Staley (No. 22). Staley was a fan favorite for his powerful running style and spent seven seasons carrying the ball out of the Eagles backfield. He rejoined the team in 2010 as a coaching intern, and over the next decade, he worked his way up in the organization and became the running backs coach as well as the assistant head coach. (Courtesy of Thomas E. Briglia/PhotoGraphics.)

The Eagles have had many excellent tight ends in their history, but one of the more underappreciated ones was Chad Lewis. Signed as an undrafted free agent in 1997, Lewis spent two seasons with the Eagles before leaving and winning a Super Bowl with Dick Vermeil's Rams. He returned to Philadelphia in 2000 and registered three consecutive Pro Bowl seasons along with an All-Pro selection. In the 2004 NFC Championship win against Atlanta, he miraculously caught a touchdown pass while breaking his foot in the process. (Courtesy of Thomas E. Briglia/PhotoGraphics.)

After losing three straight NFC Championship Games, it became evident the Eagles needed to upgrade Donovan McNabb's receiving corps. Enter Terrell Owens. The McNabb-Owens duo was unstoppable in 2004, connecting for 14 touchdowns in 14 games. Owens went down with a broken leg in week 15 but recovered in time for a two-touchdown performance in Super Bowl XXXIX. Less than a year later, Owens became entangled in a nationalized feud with both the front office and McNabb and left the team before the end of the 2005 season. (Courtesy of Thomas E. Briglia/PhotoGraphics.)

The Eagles of the early 2000s were filled with many different personalities, but one of the most hubristic was Freddie Mitchell. Philadelphia selected the wide receiver with its first-round pick in 2001, but Mitchell never lived up to his expectations. He registered just 90 receptions, 1,263 receiving yards, and 5 touchdowns in his career. That did not hinder Mitchell's ego though. He had plenty of nicknames in his four-year tenure, including "FredEx" and "The People's Champion," but he is widely known simply as "4th & 26" for his heroics in the 2004 NFC Divisional playoff game. His 28-yard reception on fourth and 26 helped force the game into overtime, where the Eagles eventually won. (Courtesy of Tom Briglia/NFL Photos.)

With 188 regular season games played in midnight green, David Akers is the longest-tenured Eagle in franchise history. Playing all of those games made it easy for Akers to set virtually every Eagles kicking record. He holds the team record for points scored (1,323), most field goals made (294) and attempted (357), most extra points made (441) and attempted (447), kickoffs (958), and kickoff yards (60,739). Akers also set a league record in 2004 when he made 17 field goals of 40-plus yards. For his accomplishments, Akers was selected to five Pro Bowl teams. (Courtesy of Thomas E. Briglia/PhotoGraphics.)

The Eagles solidified their defensive backfield in 2002 when they used their top three picks in the draft to select Lito Sheppard, Michael Lewis, and Sheldon Brown (No. 24). The Sheppard and Brown tandem at cornerback helped to guide them into Super Bowl XXXIX. Brown's most famous moment as an Eagle came in January 2007. On the opening drive of the NFC Divisional playoff game against the New Orleans Saints, Brown laid a punishing hit on Reggie Bush, who was trying to secure a catch in the backfield. (Courtesy of Thomas E. Briglia/PhotoGraphics.)

Jon Dorenbos certainly had a unique football career—from sending phony college scouting videos of him long snapping to showing off his magic tricks on a television game show. Yet after 11 seasons with the team, his most memorable moment may be his lifesaving trade to the New Orleans Saints. Dorenbos failed his physical, and the trade was voided because doctors discovered an aortic aneurysm that required immediate open-heart surgery. He fully recovered and began touring the country as a magician and a motivational speaker. (Courtesy of Thomas E. Briglia/PhotoGraphics.)

The Eagles and Baltimore Ravens refused to play the 2001 preseason opener due to the poor condition of the Veterans Stadium turf. Just two seasons later, the Vet hosted its final game, which broke Eagles fans' hearts in more ways than one. They lost the 2003 NFC Championship to the Tampa Bay Buccaneers, with the game ending on gut punch pick-six from Ronde Barber. (Courtesy of Thomas E. Briglia/PhotoGraphics.)

In 2004, the Eagles moved into Lincoln Financial Field. The $512-million stadium underwent renovations in 2013 and has an official capacity of 69,796 as of 2020. It's "Go Green" initiative made the stadium environmentally friendly, with wind turbines on the roof to generate electricity. The new stadium, along with the state-of-the-art NovaCare Complex across the street, became amenities to lure free agents and professionalize the experience for players. (Courtesy of Thomas E. Briglia/PhotoGraphics.)

Lincoln Financial Field has hosted many important and famous games, including multiple NFC Championships, the Snow Bowl, multiple Army-Navy games, the CONCACAF Gold Cup, NCAA Lacrosse Championships, and an NHL Stadium Series game. (Courtesy of Thomas E. Briglia/PhotoGraphics.)

If the words *Philadelphia Eagle* were found in the dictionary, Brent Celek's picture would be right next to them. Selected in the fifth round of the 2007 NFL draft, Celek quickly found himself as the starting tight end. He became a fan favorite for his hard-nosed mentality, as he missed only one game in his 11 seasons with the team. He recorded 398 receptions, 4,998 yards, and 31 touchdowns with the Eagles in addition to mentoring Zach Ertz. (Courtesy of Tom Briglia/ NFL Photos.)

Heading into the final day of the 2008 season, the Eagles had a slim chance of making the playoffs. After all the early games tilted in their favor, they needed to beat the Cowboys to get in. A loss meant the Cowboys would take the spot. The Eagles romped the Cowboys 44-6 and rode that moment into a long playoff run, falling just short of a possible Keystone State Super Bowl matchup against the Pittsburgh Steelers. (Courtesy of Thomas E. Briglia/PhotoGraphics.)

Drafted in the second round, DeSean Jackson made an immediate impact as an explosive down-field threat in 2008. In his first game, he racked up 203 all-purpose yards, a rookie record. In his second season, he became the first player to make the Pro Bowl at two different positions. Yet his most memorable moment was a punt return touchdown to cap off a 28-point comeback against the Giants, known as "The Miracle at the Meadowlands 2." (Courtesy of Thomas E. Briglia/PhotoGraphics.)

Andy Reid was a big believer in giving people second chances, and he made that belief clear in August 2009 when he signed Michael Vick. The signing of Vick was met with controversy, as he was just released from prison a month earlier after serving time for being a part of a dog fighting organization. He spent his first season in Philadelphia mostly on the sidelines, but his big break came in week one of 2010. Slated to be the backup quarterback, Vick was thrown into action when Kevin Kolb suffered a concussion. He never let go of that starting job as he led the Eagles offense to one of its best seasons of the 21st century. His signature moment came in the "Monday Night Massacre," in which he became the first player in NFL history to have more than 300 passing yards, 50-plus rushing yards, 4-plus passing touchdowns, and 2-plus rushing touchdowns in the same game. (Courtesy of Thomas E. Briglia/PhotoGraphics.)

Other notable players from 1997 to 2012 include guard Evan Mathis (No. 69), linebacker Ike Reese, tackle Jon Runyan, cornerback Troy Vincent, cornerback Bobby Taylor, cornerback Lito Shepard, linebacker Jeremiah Trotter, defensive end Hugh Douglas, defensive end Trent Cole, cornerback Asante Samuel, guard Jermane Mayberry, defensive tackle Corey Simon, safety Quintin Mikell, safety Michael Lewis, fullback Leonard Weaver, guard Shawn Andrews, and tackle Tra Thomas. (Courtesy of Tom Briglia/NFL Photos.)

The Eagles tradition of successful running backs carried over into the 2010s when LeSean "Shady" McCoy came to town. As a second-round pick in the 2009 NFL draft, he spent his rookie season learning from Brian Westbrook then took over the reins in 2010. He was the league rushing touchdown leader in 2011 and rushing yards leader in 2013 and in the process became a perennial Pro Bowler as well as a two-time All-Pro selection. He was unceremoniously traded to Buffalo in 2015 when head coach Chip Kelly won an internal power struggle with general manager Howie Roseman. His 6,792 rushing yards are a franchise record. (Courtesy of Thomas E. Briglia/PhotoGraphics.)

6

ROAD TO GLORY

2013–2019

Even though the Eagles were Super Bowl contenders for over a decade in the 2000s under Andy Reid, the team was never able to achieve that ultimate goal Eagles fans had been starving for across several generations. The time felt right for Eagles owner Jeffrey Lurie to finally divorce from the longest-tenured coach in team history after the team's final game in 2012. The search for a new head coach who could help the Eagles win their first Super Bowl was underway.

The franchise looked outside the box for its next hire and decided to bring in college football's most innovative coach, Chip Kelly, to Philadelphia to see if his offensive style of coaching could revolutionize the NFL. His first season was a smashing success that resulted in a division title, and with Kelly receiving constant praise from personnel across the league, it seemed like the Eagles would at least keep their status as perennial Super Bowl contenders. Then in a blink of an eye, the Kelly experiment came crashing down as a front office power struggle emerged. Kelly won the battle for control over team personnel in 2015 but ultimately lost the war, as his team finished 6-10 and Lurie fired him before the conclusion of the season. The team was now searching for its third head coach in five years.

Doug Pederson, a former Eagles quarterback and a protégé of Andy Reid in Kansas City, was selected as the next head coach in Philadelphia. Howie Roseman was handed back the general manager duties, and from there, the decision was made to invest in a franchise quarterback. The team traded up to select Carson Wentz second overall in 2016. With a series of successful free agent additions and draft selections, the team finally had the right ingredients for its first Super Bowl victory.

Chip Kelly was expected to bring a revolutionary, fast-paced, and high-scoring offense when he came to the Eagles from the University of Oregon. He did just that in his first season, when he helped lead the team to the 2013 division title. (Courtesy of Thomas E. Briglia/PhotoGraphics.)

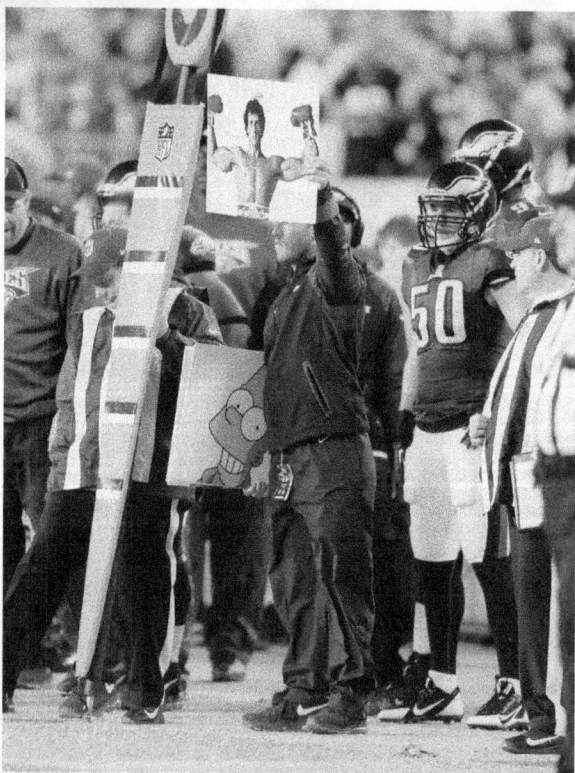

Chip Kelly's initial success ultimately resulted in his demise. A big boost to Kelly's ego led to a power struggle with Howie Roseman for general manager duties, which Kelly won. By 2015, Kelly got rid of multiple star players, including DeSean Jackson and LeSean McCoy. The players he brought in to replace them could not reproduce the production lost, and Kelly was fired before the 2015 season finale. (Courtesy of Thomas E. Briglia/PhotoGraphics.)

By the end of the 2016 season, Kelly was out of the NFL entirely, and Howie Roseman returned as a man on a mission. He traded up in the 2016 draft to select Carson Wentz and was named Pro Football Writers of America Executive of the Year after the 2017 season. He is standing here with defensive coordinator Jim Schwartz (2016–2020). (Courtesy of John Jones/ Icon Sportswire.)

One of the most memorable games in the history of Lincoln Financial Field took place on December 8, 2013. The pregame flurries turned blizzard-like once the Eagles and Lions kicked off. The Eagles scored 28 points in the fourth quarter to secure a 34-20 win behind LeSean McCoy's franchise record 217 rushing yards. (Courtesy of Ed Mahan.)

The hiring of Doug Pederson in 2016 was met with much scrutiny due to his lack of head coaching experience. The Andy Reid protégé created a close-knit locker room, which was a big reason for the success that came in 2017. His aggressive game management vaulted the Eagles to the top seed in the NFC playoffs. He ended up becoming the eighth head coach in NFL history to win the Super Bowl within his first two seasons as a head coach as well as the seventh head coach to win the Super Bowl in his first playoff run. (Courtesy of Ray Carlin/Icon Sportswire.)

The Eagles selected Carson Wentz with the second overall pick in the 2016 NFL draft. After a promising rookie campaign, Wentz exploded in 2017. He set the Eagles franchise record for passing touchdowns in a season (33). The last one thrown that season was on a torn ACL, as Wentz hurt his knee a few plays earlier and refused to leave the game until he finished the drive. He led the team to an 11-2 record before suffering the injury, a record that helped secure home-field advantage in the postseason. (Courtesy of Thomas E. Briglia/PhotoGraphics.)

Nick Foles's time in Philadelphia can only be described as chaotic. He took the league by storm in 2013 when he replaced an injured Michael Vick. That year he tied the league record with seven passing touchdowns in one game and also became the first Eagles quarterback to lead the league in passer rating (119.2) since Tommy Thompson. Foles failed to live up to the hype in 2014 and was traded the following off-season to the St. Louis Rams for Sam Bradford. He made his return to Philadelphia in 2017 to serve as backup to Carson Wentz. When Wentz suffered a season-ending injury in week 14, Foles stepped up once again and led an improbable run that resulted in the team's first Super Bowl victory, becoming just the eighth backup quarterback in NFL history to lead his team to a Super Bowl win. (Courtesy of Thomas E. Briglia/PhotoGraphics.)

There were a few similarities between the 1960 NFL Championship Eagles team and the 2017 Eagles. The biggest one came from game-winning kicks. In 1960, Bobby Walson's last-second kick put the Eagles on top of the Cleveland Browns in week five. That win gave Eagles fans hope that a special season was coming. History repeated itself when Jake Elliott lined up for a 61-yard field goal as time expired in the week three game against the New York Giants. Elliott's kick was successful and put him in the Eagles record book for the longest field goal in franchise history. That kick became the catalyst for the team that season, and it gave fans the feeling that a special season was about to take place. (Courtesy of Andy Lewis/Icon Sportswire.)

As a free agent signing in 2014, Malcolm Jenkins made an instant impact on the field and was named to the Pro Bowl three times while with the Eagles. His intense leadership—similar in style to Brian Dawkins and crucial in the team's Super Bowl run—was summed up in his motto, "We all we got. We all we need." (Courtesy of Kyle Ross/Icon Sportswire.)

The Eagles had a hard time finding a star defensive tackle following Jerome Brown's tragic death, but the team finally struck gold when it traded up for Fletcher Cox in the 2012 NFL draft. His excellence in both pass rushing and run stopping has earned him six Pro Bowl trips and four All-Pro teams; he was also named to the 2010s All-Decade Team. As of 2021, his 54.5 sacks are the most by an interior lineman in team history. (Courtesy of Kyle Ross/Icon Sportswire.)

One of the best trades in Eagles history was when Andy Reid acquired Jason Peters (right) from the Buffalo Bills in 2009. Even though he battled multiple serious injuries in an Eagles uniform, his 148 games played are the 13th most in franchise history. His nine Pro Bowl nominations and six All-Pro selections likely mean Peters will one day be enshrined into the Pro Football Hall of Fame. (Courtesy of Andy Lewis/Icon Sportswire.)

Chris Long donned the "Underdog Mask" after the Eagles defeated the favored Atlanta Falcons in the 2017 divisional round of the playoffs. The masks became a massive trend throughout the city of Philadelphia, so he and Lane Johnson continued to wear them during the memorable playoff run. The season was especially rewarding for Long, as he had donated his entire 2017 base salary, worth $1 million, to charity. The following season, he was selected as the 2018 Walter Payton NFL Man of the Year, becoming the second Eagle to win the prestigious award. (Courtesy of Andy Lewis/Icon Sportswire.)

The aftermath of the 38-7 NFC Championship Game win over the Vikings is seen here, setting the stage for the Eagles' third Super Bowl appearance. The 2017 Eagles used team chemistry to overcome adversity. Notable players on offense include LeGarrette Blount, Jay Ajayi, Nelson Agholor, Torrey Smith, and Alshon Jeffery and on defense Vinny Curry, Patrick Robinson, and Timmy Jernigan. (Courtesy of Elliott Gaskins.)

Near the end of the second quarter of the Super Bowl, on fourth down with the Eagles at the Patriots one-yard line, Nick Foles suggested—and Doug Pederson called—one of the gutsiest plays in team history. Executed to perfection, the "Philly Special" or "Philly Philly" called for a direct snap to running back Corey Clement (from Glassboro, New Jersey), a pitch to tight end Trey Burton, then a pass to quarterback Nick Foles. (Courtesy of Nick Wosika/Icon Sportswire.)

Drafted in the second round of the 2013 draft, Zach Ertz was soon one of the best tight ends in the league, earning three Pro Bowl nods. He became a household name nationwide when he scored the dramatic game-winning touchdown of Super Bowl LII. He followed his impressive Super Bowl performance the next season by setting the NFL record for most receptions by a tight end with 116. (Courtesy of Rich Graessle/Icon Sportswire.)

THE PHILADELPHIA EAGLES

Brandon Graham was initially labeled a draft bust, but the determined defensive end wanted to prove everyone wrong. His hard work and constantly running motor have made him an Eagles legend. He cemented his legacy in Super Bowl LII when he caused a strip sack of Tom Brady late in the fourth quarter, which all but sealed the team's first championship in 57 years. He now reigns as the longest-tenured defensive lineman in team history. (Courtesy of Nick Wosika/ Icon Sportswire.)

When the victorious Eagles returned home, the city was ecstatic. During the subsequent parade, Jason Kelce borrowed a police bicycle so that he could ride around and greet as many Eagles fans as possible. His green and purple sequin outfit paid tribute to the famous Philadelphia Mummers tradition. (Courtesy of Mike Dillon.)

Corey Clement and Jay Ajayi give high fives to Eagles fans as they pass them along the Super Bowl parade route on Broad Street. In the bus behind them, the players show off a super-sized Lombardi Trophy made by a fan. (Courtesy of Sybil Katona.)

Here, Doug Pederson is shown hoisting the Lombardi Trophy next to Howie Roseman. As the buses processed up Broad Street, fans on both sides repeatedly tossed cans of beer to the players and coaches. (Courtesy of Barbara Barnes.)

The victory parade started outside of Lincoln Financial Field and worked its way up Broad Street. Once it reached city hall, it then made its way across the Benjamin Franklin Parkway before ending on the Philadelphia Museum of Art steps. While on the famous steps, many of the team's leaders gave passionate speeches thanking fans for their support. (Above, courtesy of Bob Novak; below, courtesy of Thomas E. Briglia/PhotoGraphics.)

A Philadelphia Eagles parade float filled with players, team staff, and family members passes by waves of fans on Broad Street on February 8, 2018. The Eagles were celebrating their first Super Bowl victory in franchise history, in which they defeated the New England Patriots 41-33 in Super Bowl LII just four days earlier in Minneapolis, Minnesota. (Photograph by Andrew Weicker.)

While on the art museum steps, Jason Kelce provided a rambling and profanity-laden speech that whipped the mass of Eagles fans into a frenzy. Two famous phrases from his speech are often quoted by fans: "Hungry dogs run faster" and "No one likes us, we don't care." (Courtesy of Ricky Fitchett/Zuma Press/Icon Sportswire.)

The Eagles unveiled their first Super Bowl banner at a packed Lincoln Financial Field to kick off the 2018 season. They kept their winning streak going, beating the Falcons 18-12. (Courtesy of Thomas E. Briglia/PhotoGraphics.)

A "Philly Special" statue was unveiled before the team kicked off their season opener. The statue commemorated the famous moment that took place in Super Bowl LII, where quarterback Nick Foles asked head coach Doug Pederson, "You want Philly Philly?," referring to the trick play the team had practiced where Foles would become a receiver rather than a quarterback. Pederson's reply, "Yeah, let's do it," allowed the play to commence, which is now debated as the best trick play in Super Bowl history. (Courtesy of Bob Novak.)

7

THROUGH THE YEARS
FAN PHOTOGRAPHS

Eagles fans are as loyal as they come. Yes, they are loud and aggressive, but their reputation belies a fierce loyalty based in love. Hard-nosed, skilled players who are dedicated to the team are rewarded with godlike status. Just ask Chuck Bednarik, Tommy McDonald, Reggie White, and Brian Dawkins: Inspiration is a two-way street.

Success has not knocked often on the door of Eagles fans. There have been more dysfunctional owners than dynasties, and the seasons between 1961 and 2000 were usually filled with disappointment. So unfortunately, the stories are true. Snowballs were indeed thrown at an inebriated replacement Santa in 1968. Effigies of coach Joe Kuharich were no doubt hung on Franklin Field flagpoles. And yes, a courtroom was installed in the basement of Veterans Stadium because the upper level was so rowdy. So the reputation is well deserved, but it does tend to overshadow the positive aspects of Eagles fandom.

Eagles fan travel as much as, or more than, any other fanbase. Cities hosting Eagles away games instantly become awash in green thanks to groups like Philly Sports Trips and the legendary Green Legion. This enhanced perspective is supplemented by a long history of media greats. Storytellers like By Saam, Bill Campbell, Ray Didinger, and Merrill Reese have helped to create generations of knowledgeable fans.

Once in a while, all the dedication and early morning tailgates pay off. The Eagles won back-to-back NFL Championships in 1948 and 1949, then another in 1960. But after the AFL–NFL merger in 1966, the newly minted Super Bowl eluded the Birds for half a century. Finally, Eagles fans around the world were rewarded on February 4, 2018, with their first Super Bowl victory. The impromptu celebrations broke out up and down Broad Street, at Frankford and Cottman Avenues, and all over the Delaware Valley. The parade in 2018 was a cold, cathartic experience—one not soon to be forgotten!

Before professional football, crowds flocked to the amateur games around Philadelphia. Here, fans fill the stadium to capacity for a gridiron game around 1900. (Photograph by Franklin Davenport Edmunds; courtesy of Free Library of Philadelphia.)

Fans are dressed to watch a Yellow Jackets game in 1926 at Frankford Stadium. It was mostly men who would show up to cheer on the Yellow Jackets, and instead of wearing jerseys and team colors that are common these days, the attire was "Sunday's best," even though games at the time were not allowed on Sundays due to the Pennsylvania blue laws. (Courtesy of Frankford Historical Society.)

Yellow Jackets fans did not get as rowdy as Eagles fans, but they still had the same amount of passion for the team. The stands were always crowded in Northeast Philadelphia to watch professional football. (Courtesy of Frankford Historical Society.)

The wives of Joe Carter, Swede Hansen, and Art Buss cheer on their husbands during an intrasquad scrimmage in the early days of Eagles football. (Courtesy of the Historical Society of Pennsylvania.)

This award-winning photograph shows unruly fans being apprehended by police on Franklin Field after the Eagles won the NFL Championship in 1960. Little did these Eagles fans know that they would not be able to express excitement after a championship win again for another 57 years. (Courtesy of Temple University Libraries.)

After the 1980 NFC Championship win over Dallas, an overzealous fan is captured as he elbows Dick Vermeil in the face during an impromptu on-field celebration. Even the incidental contact could not wipe the smile from Vermeil's face as he realized he was finally heading to a Super Bowl. (Courtesy of Ed Mahan.)

The initial incident that gave Eagles fans their bad name was throwing snowballs at Santa Claus in 1968. Former Philadelphia mayor and Pennsylvania governor Ed Rendell was among those in attendance for that game. He remembered fans being disgruntled during the final game of the season since the team had only won two games so far. A halftime show had to use a replacement Santa since the original was sick, and his performance was inadequate at best. Eagles fans took out their frustrations by pummeling the faux Santa with snowballs. (Courtesy of Philadelphia Evening Bulletin Collection, Temple University Libraries.)

The 700 Level inside of Veterans Stadium became notorious due to the unruly and rowdy Eagles fans that would sit in the nosebleed sections. In 1986, the team stopped selling beer after halftime and requested the NFL to not schedule 4:00 p.m. games at the Vet against rivals in hopes alcohol consumption would decrease. Fan behavior gained national attention after a 1997 Monday night football game that saw 60 reported fistfights in the stands and a flare gun being fired by a fan into an empty section of the stadium. It was decided the following season that a functioning court needed to be added beneath the stadium. Judge Seamus McCaffery was the judge at "Eagles Court" and later became a Pennsylvania Supreme Court judge. (Courtesy of Thomas E. Briglia/PhotoGraphics.)

Philadelphians arrive at Frankford Stadium for a Yellow Jackets game. Previously, blue laws prohibited the sales of alcohol and even games on Sundays in Philadelphia. Many teams would travel to Frankford for a game on Saturday then the next day play in Pottsville, where enforcement was relaxed. (Courtesy of the Frankford Historical Society.)

Tailgating before games in the parking lots surrounding Lincoln Financial Field has become a pregame ritual since the Eagles moved to South Philadelphia. Families and friends make the trek down to the sports stadium complex with cold drinks and hot food and kill time before kickoff by playing games like cornhole or previewing the upcoming game and talking strategy about the incoming opponent. (Courtesy of Philly Sports Trips.)

Eagles fans have a bad reputation that is not undeserved, but it does overshadow the good that fans can do. Since May 2018, Eagles fans have donated over $10 million to the Eagles Autism Challenge. (Courtesy of the Green Legion.)

Thanks to fan travel groups like the Green Legion, every road game still feels like it is being played inside of Lincoln Financial Field. Even for the playoffs, thousands of Eagles fans made their way down to the New Orleans Superdome to cheer on the team as it faced the Saints. (Courtesy of the Green Legion.)

A beautiful California sunset takes place at the Los Angeles Coliseum as the Eagles faced the Los Angeles Rams in a late-2017 matchup. Eagles fans packed the coliseum. Even though the Eagles ended up winning that game, fans in attendance (and those watching from home) were more concerned about Carson Wentz, who left the game early with what turned out to be a season-ending ACL injury. (Courtesy of Jenny Pina.)

Eagles fans traveled to London in October 2018 to see their team play its first international regular season game against the Jacksonville Jaguars at Wembley Stadium. Many of the 85,870 in attendance wore midnight green to support their favorite team overseas. The Eagles rewarded the fans who made the long flight over, as they held on for a 24-18 victory. (Courtesy of Lisa Fazio.)

The night the Philadelphia Eagles won their first Super Bowl on February 4, 2018, celebrations broke out all across the Delaware Valley, none livelier than the euphoria from the thousands of Eagles fans that converged along Broad Street. The longest street in Philadelphia was illuminated with green lights and fireworks that stretched all the way to city hall. (Courtesy of Lauren McLaughlin.)

All of Broad Street became a sea of green once the game clock hit 00:00 on Super Bowl LII. Fans made their way out of their homes and out of the bars to head toward city hall to celebrate the big victory in the heart of the city. (Courtesy of Joe Cramphorn.)

Fans put on their best Eagles jerseys and costumes when they went to Broad Street for the team's Super Bowl LII parade. Many schools and businesses gave their students and employees the day off so they could witness the historic event in person. (Courtesy of Bob Novak.)

A mass of Eagles fans are walking along the Benjamin Franklin Parkway on the day of the Eagles' Super Bowl LII parade. Crowd safety experts estimated that there were 700,000 people in attendance for the parade, but many believe the actual number was in the millions. (Courtesy of Bob Novak.)

Thirteen busts of former Philadelphia Eagles players that are enshrined into the Pro Football Hall of Fame were on display at Lincoln Financial Field while the Eagles faced the Carolina Panthers on October 21, 2018. The busts were brought from Canton, Ohio (home of the Pro Football Hall of Fame), to celebrate Eagles legend Brian Dawkins, who was enshrined on August 4, 2018. Dawkins's bust can be seen in the first row, third from the left. (Courtesy of Andrew Weicker.)

Eagles cheerleaders were first introduced in 1948. The cheerleaders were known as the Eaglettes through the 1970s. Then for the next decade, they were known as the Liberty Belles. Today, they are simply called the Philadelphia Eagles Cheerleaders. (Courtesy of Ed Mahan.)

Philadelphia cheerleaders lined up at the 1981 Thanksgiving Day Parade in front of the famed Philadelphia Museum of Art steps. The cheerleaders help bring football to a full circle in the city; while the city's professional football team has its cheerleaders performing on Thanksgiving, there is plenty of football being played across the region by the local high schools with historic rivalries. (Photograph by Michael G. Spafford.)

Eagles cheerleaders can put every Eagles fan in a good mood no matter what is happening in the game. (Courtesy of Thomas E. Briglia/PhotoGraphics.)

"Fly Eagles Fly" is the anthem sung by fans after touchdowns, wins, and important life events. Written by Charles Borrelli in the 1950s and often performed by the Eagles' official marching band, the Sound of Brass, it was forgotten after Leonard Tose bought the team and broke up the band. (Courtesy of Peter Capolino.)

The Eagles fight song originally was called "Fight, Eagles, Fight." When Jeffrey Lurie took over as owner, he revived the song, and it was altered to the chant that every Eagles fan now knows by heart. (Courtesy of Andrew Palagruto.)

There have been many famous broadcasters and media members associated with the Eagles through the years. Here Shibe Park public address announcer Sherry O'Brien calls a game with his spotters. Fans will also recall the voices of Byrum Saam, Bill Campbell, and Andy Musser calling games for WCAU radio and writers such as Art Morrow, Jack McKinney, Hugh Brown, and Ray Didinger. (Courtesy of Ed Mahan.)

Known as the voice of the Eagles, Merrill Reese (right) has been the team's play-by-play announcer on the radio since 1977, making him the longest-serving current play-by-play announcer in the NFL. In recognition for his dedication to the team, he was enshrined into the Eagles Hall of Fame in 2016. (Courtesy of Ed Mahan.)

Ray Didinger's fandom as a child blossomed into a hall of fame sports writing career and playwright of *Tommy and Me*—the story of young Ray meeting Tommy McDonald at training camp then later leading the campaign to enshrine McDonald in the hall of fame. Here they are at a birthday celebration for Steve Van Buren (seated, center) along with (left to right) Ken Farragut, Tommy, Ray, Pete Retzlaff, Jim Gallagher, and Chuck Bednarik. (Courtesy of Ray Didinger.)

Bill Bergey is seen stretching actor John Travolta. Travolta injured his leg while filming the 1981 film *Blow Out* in Philadelphia and came to the Eagles' facility for their high-performance orthopedic treatments. (Courtesy of Ed Mahan.)

THE PHILADELPHIA EAGLES

One of the most die-hard celebrity Eagles fans is Sylvester Stallone, who famously played Philadelphia boxer Rocky in the successful titular movie franchise. Other A-list celebrity Eagles fans include Will Smith, Kevin Hart, and Mike Trout. Trout is a season ticket holder and is constantly spotted at regular season games. (Courtesy of Thomas E. Briglia/PhotoGraphics.)

Bradley Cooper took a picture with former vice president Joe Biden and his wife, Dr. Jill Biden, prior to Super Bowl LII. Joe Biden is the first Eagles fan in history to become president of the United States when he won the election in 2020. (Courtesy of Jill Biden.)

In 1996, the Eagles officially named Swoop their mascot. Though occasionally overshadowed by the city's other famous mascots, like the Phillie Phanatic and Gritty, Swoop has remained a popular figure associated with the franchise. (Courtesy of Thomas E. Briglia/PhotoGraphics.)

Philadelphia sporting events were electric in the early 1980s. All four major sports teams (Eagles, Sixers, Flyers, and Phillies) made the playoffs in 1980, and three of them made their respective championship games. It was a great time to be a fan in Philadelphia. (Courtesy of Ed Mahan.)

Visit us at
arcadiapublishing.com

www.ingramcontent.com/pod-product-compliance
Lightning Source LLC
Chambersburg PA
CBHW070412100426
42812CB00005B/1721